THE

FORGOTTEN

AMERICANS

CHARLOTTE TRINCHIERI WARD

www.happyselfpublisher.com

TABLE OF CONTENTS

❧

FAMILY TRINCHIERI

Long before that wartime encounter, let me tell my family story. My grandfather on my father's side was Carlo di Trinchieri born in Bene Vagienna, Italy in December 1855. His father was an Italian Count. He married my grandmother, Marie Tisseur in 1881. They celebrated their honeymoon on the Riviera in Nizza, (now Nice, France). My aunt Josephine was born in Nice on November 4, 1882. My uncle Louis was born in Genoa, Italy on July 12, 1887. My grandparents immigrated to the United States with their children in 1891 where they lived in Manhattan on Christopher Street. My aunt Jeannette was born there on July 2, 1891 and my father Felix on June 12, 1897. While living in New York, they owned two restaurants: the Cavour Club and The Lafayette Club. Later, they bought one square mile of property in Ringwood Junction, New Jersey where they had a resort hotel. In the early movie years, the French film company Paté-Frères made films on their property and Pancho Villa, the feather-weight champion trained there. Lake Josephine on the New

Jersey map was named after my aunt. My half-sister Jeannine was born in New Jersey, on July 24. 1921. Her mother left to live in France. Two years later, my father married my mother Mary Tirozzi who was born in Paterson, New Jersey on January 27, 1898. In 1927, the county of Passaic forced my grandparents to sell the land prior to the building of the Wanaque reservoir. It was then that the family decided to move and live in Nice, France. My father Felix, my mother Mary, my half-sister Jeannine, my aunt Josephine and my aunt Jeannette followed them, but my uncle Louis remained.

Villa Trinchieri nestled in a hill of Ringwood Junction, New Jersey

Lake Josephine

NICE, FRANCE

❧

I was born at 10:30 a.m. on April 26, 1936 in Nice in the "Villa Trinchieri," one of the most beautiful homes of the neighborhood. We overlooked the town and the Mediterranean. It was a white stone stucco house with green shutters, sun porches and terraces.

A wall topped with a hedge surrounded the property. In the garden, there were at least 40 fruit trees. Among them were fig, persimmon, orange, tangerine, lemon, plum, cherry and apricot trees.

The flowers and cactus plants perfumed the garden and brightened our path. Inside the house, the French windows were always open to let in the sparkling rays of sun and the occasional twitter of the robins that lived in our cherry tree. When the sun was too bright, we either closed the shutters completely or kept open the middle section. Although there was central heating, every room had a fireplace. The kitchen and the bathrooms had marble floors, and all the rooms had parquet floors covered with burgundy red woolen area rugs embellished with lighter shades of roses in full bloom.

Years later, I asked my father what kind of day it was when I was born. He said, "It was beautiful. The trees were budding and the palm leaves were softly rustling beneath the deep blue Mediterranean sky. When Doctor Chatenoux came to deliver you, he stopped to admire the pink and yellow sweet smelling roses already in bloom."

Before the war, we were living a luxurious life. We had a maid and a gardener. Our Italian maid, Margarita, and her husband lived at the house. Although Margarita helped in the kitchen, the cooking was primarily done by my grandmother and the baking was done by my Aunt Josephine.

More than anything else, I miss my home. I miss it so much that I often dream about it. I would like to describe it to your now. As you entered the locked gate of the villa the stairs leading to the garden were on the left side.

First, I would like to take you to the lower garden on the seaside of the house. From these stairs, you could see the garage. In the garage was a Buick Town car brought to France from the United States. I thought it was a great looking car. One day, my Jeannine said to me, "Je n'aime pas cette voiture! Quand papa vient me chercher à l'école j'ai honte parce que les parents de mes amis ont des voitures modernes." ("I don't like this car! When dad picks me up at school I'm ashamed because the parents of my friends have modern cars.")

As you stepped down these stairs on the right was a small garden with an apricot tree surrounded with lilies of the valley and a rose bush. There was a concrete patio stretching all the way across to the other side of the property. Along the house facing the garden was a green wrought iron table with an umbrella and matching chairs. There were also two lounge chairs with stripped green and white cushions. Clinging to the wall of the house behind the patio furniture were vines of purple bougainvillea. It was very pleasant to sit there in full view of varied colored geraniums, fruit trees and the vegetable garden. On a hot day, we would sip freshly squeezed lemonade. The French have a special way of presenting the lemonade. One pitcher is filled with the lemon juice, another one with ice water. There is also a bucket of ice and a sugar bowl. Each person fills their glass with the combination that pleases them.

The garden itself was made up of parterres of various shapes surrounded by white pebbles. On the left side against the wall of the property was a raised garden held by a retaining wall. In it were large cactus plants which bore yellow flowers. The first parterre was a long rectangular area filled with orange trees. The fruits were not sprayed with pesticides; therefore, we were able to make orange fritters by dipping the segments of the orange peels into a batter, frying them, and while they were hot, we would sprinkle them with sugar.

Alongside the orange tree garden was a large circle surrounded by four kidney shaped gardens. It was there that we planted tangerine and lemon trees. Next, was another large rectangle with a plum tree in the middle which was surrounded with vegetables: various salads, fennels, tomatoes, peppers, eggplants, onions and cardoons: a vegetable of the artichoke family. After removing the stringy parts from the tender stalks, we would cut the cardoons in three-inch-long slices. The slices were cooked in a court-bouillon, drained and covered with a sauce made of anchovies, olive oil and garlic. I enjoyed picking the Italian red or yellow tomatoes and eating them while they were still warm. I also liked the taste of baked tomatoes filled with a mixture of olive oil, fresh basil, parsley, garlic and bread crumbs. These were baked in the oven. The tomatoes, eggplants, zucchinis and onions were sometimes made into a ratatouille. The fennels were delicious cooked in the oven with a roast beef.

Next to the vegetable garden was a smaller rectangle with a cherry tree on one end and a white fig tree on the other. Potatoes and zucchini were planted there. Another unusual delicacy for me were the fritters made with the zucchini flowers. After removing the stamens four to six flowers were placed inside each other and coated with a batter made from milk, eggs, flour salt and pepper. Then they were sautéed in olive oil.

Two tall medlar trees were next to the wall of the property which separated us from our neighbors. The yellow fruit called 'nèfle' is about three inches in diameter. My favorite place to sit was in the hidden garden located to the right of the second staircase. The entrance to this garden was flanked by two symmetrical round privet bushes. My father, who was proud to be an American citizen, clipped the letters U.S.A. on them. A tree bearing large purple figs was so tall that it reached the balcony of the upper patio. In the Spring, the garden was very private when it was covered with a harbor of pink roses. Against the far wall was a green iron bench. In front of it were two matching chairs and a round table. It was my favorite place to play with my dolls or have lunch with my two friends Daniel and Maurice. Since there were many places to hide in the garden, we often played 'Hide and seek'. From the patio, I could see the house next door. Our properties were separated by a low wall on the left of which there were stairs and a gate so we could visit. My half-sister's friend Simone lived there. Jeannine and Simone had two mutual friends: Jaqueline and Nicole. Jacqueline lived near our apartment building and Nicole lived in town. One day while I

8

was picking our sweet-smelling violets, I heard Simone calling me. She said, "Viens, j'ai un petit cadeau pour toi." ("Come, I have a little present for you.") I climbed the stairs and opened the gate. She was holding the present behind her back. "Tiens," she said. ("Here," she said.") She handed me a tiny beige wicker baby carriage with a one inch doll inside. "Que c'est joli, merci." ("It's so pretty, thank you.") I said. I hugged her and ran back to the house to show everyone my special treasure. I then returned to the garden to pick more violets. I loved to pick them and arrange them in a special globe shaped vase with small holes which allowed the delicate flowers to stand up.

Upon entering through the gate, straight ahead and to the right were the steps leading to the house. There was a roof over the landing and from the ceiling hung a stained glass multicolored lamp. The large double wooden oak doors had two windows on the inside which could be opened to let in the breeze or to see who was at the gate ringing the doorbell.

The front door opened to a large marble hallway where we used to dance to the music of records played on an R.C.A. Victor record player that had a handle on the side used to wind up the turning table. There were two louvered doors in the front which when opened increased the sound of the music. The records were stored in the cabinet below. I often danced Strauss waltzes with my dad. In those days, women wore long dresses for dances. I still remember the dresses flowing with the beat of the music. The hall was lit with a crystal chandelier which reflected in the mirror on the back wall.

Off the hall was a room which used to be the study, but became the bedroom for my mother and me. Upon opening the door, the dressing table was on the left. I was always fascinated by the sight of the perfume bottles and makeup my mother had.

One day, when my mother was shopping, I took powder, rouge, lipstick and eye shadow from the dressing table applied them to my face. When my mother came home she said, "Mon Dieu, qu'est-ce que tu as fait?" ("My God, what did you do?") Then she added, "Va te laver la figure. Tu es trop jeune pour te maquiller!" ("Go wash your face. You are too young to be wearing makeup!") I wonder if this is the reason that even to this day, I hardly wear make-up!

My bed was on the left corner of the room and above it was a built-in closet in which there were books for me written in French. My mother used to read them to me before I went to sleep. I loved the short stories in the book Lettres de mon Moulin by Alponse Daudet. My favorite one was about the goats who liked to run away to the mountains. She also read the book Pinocchio by Carlo Collodi. Geppetto created a wooden puppet who wanted to be a real boy. Whenever Geppetto lied, his nose would grow long. When I was nine years, old the Deschamps family gave me the book Seulette by Pierre Maël and Le Bon Petit Diable by the Countess de Ségur. Seulette is the story of an orphan and Le Bon Petit Diable was about a mischevious little boy who was paddled by his caretaker. He painted a devil on his underwear. The next time the caretaker pulled down his pants to paddle him she was so frightened by the sight of the devil that she never hit him again. There was a strange book in the closet which showed pictures of funeral wreaths. Since I couldn't read, I just sat in my bed turning the pages and enjoying the beauty of the flowers. Against the wall next to my bed was a fireplace with a light blue marble mantel. On top of the mantle was an antique beige porcelain clock with pretty flowers. My mother's bed was on the right side of the room facing the fireplace. On one side of her bed was a night stand and a lamp and on the other side to the right of the window was a sink and a bidet. When I was very little, I was bathed in this bidet. To the left of the window was a large armoire. It was in this room that I cut off all the long English curls of my doll. On Christmas Eve, I had to go to bed early. I was told that Santa would not come if I didn't go to bed. Sometimes when I was in bed trying to sleep, I could hear the friends of my family saying goodnight. They were lenthy goodnights; it seemed the conversations went on forever. One night, one of the friends said, "Je vous souhaite les cinq lettres." ("I wish you the five letters.") The next day, I asked what that meant. I was told that they were wishing them good luck. They were too polite to say the word "merde" which means "shit". The idea was that if you stepped in shit, you were supposed to have good luck.

Across the hall from my room were two double French doors. On the wall between them was a rose silk wall hanging embroidered with the Chinese words long life. This type of tapestry was usually displayed during a birthday celebration. The door to the left led to the living room. It was furnished with a brocaded Louis XVI settee and matching chairs. The piano was on the left corner of the room. It had built in brass candelabras on both sides. On the wall above it hung a French tapestry representing a painting by Rubens called "Lunch on the grass". On the right, there was a Chinese painting showing people climbing narrow mountain roads riding on donkeys. Next to the painting was the fireplace adorned with a light green marble mantle. The mantle was adorned with a Louis XVI clock and matching urns. Next to the fireplace was another Chinese painting representing Spring. The settee was in the corner of the room next to the window which was draped with ecru hand crocheted lace curtains. In the middle of the room was a small table on which there was a bone colored vase embossed with beautiful ladies wearing togas. It was always filled with fresh roses or carnations. The chairs were placed around the room in full view of the piano. On the left corner facing the dining room was a white marble pedestal on which was my favorite statue. It was a white marble sculpture of the Virgin Mary wearing a long flowing dress. She was holding baby Jesus in her arms. He was holding up the index and the middle finger which is the sign of peace.

It was in this room that I would often fall asleep on the soft woolen rug as I listened to my Aunt Jeannette playing the piano as she did her vocal exercises. Our entire family enjoyed music. Both my aunts had studied music at Julliard. My aunt Josephine was a coloratura soprano, played the violin and the mandolin. My Aunt Jeannette was a dramatic soprano. My half-sister Jeannine practiced the piano every day, and I came to enjoy classical music. Once a week, the family would get together with the Deschamps family who played the violin, the piano and the cello. Although I learned to play the piano, I was never a performer. I preferred sitting at the piano with a box of music by my side, playing one semi-classical piece after another for pleasure. Because I was exposed to music every day, I later developed an interest in writing poetry with social themes which I set to music. The living room connected to the large dining room via folding French doors. On the right corner of the dining room was a small table on which was the radio. Every day I would say to my dad, "Tu veux écouter la radio avec moi?" ("Do you want to listen to the radio with me?") He never said no. I would cuddle in his arms while we enjoyed the music. On the left side of the room were two windows facing the garden. The crocheted curtains flowed to the floor. In front of each window were two black and white marble pedestals on which stood bronze statues of women. One of them was holding a cornucopia. Between these windows was a fireplace with a rose mantle on which rested a French black marble and bronze clock flanked on either sided by two black marble angels holding bronze candelabras. On the wall behind the mantle hung a French gilt mirror which reflected the crystal chandelier and the china closet. The dining room table, which sat twelve people comfortably, was located in the middle of the room under the chandelier. It was always adorned with a bouquet of fresh flowers, because we always ate our main meals there. The three meals in French were: le petit déjeuner, le déjeuner and le souper. Students were allowed to go home for the déjeuner which for us was the main meal.

On the other end of room, two Morris chairs with green velvet cushions faced each other. One was for my grandma and the other for my grandpa. They sat there every day to read the newspapers. There was another china closet on the far wall. Under it was a shelf filled with large colorful seas hells. I loved to press the conch shell against my ear to hear the sound of the sea! Large pastoral paintings with guilt frames decorated the room. In the far left corner was a door leading to a sitting room.

We gathered around the dining room table for hours especially when we had guests. For special holidays, we always invited the Deschamps. The Deschamps family consisted of Alice who was married to André, Germaine and Lucille, her sisters. They all lived together in a house situated up the steep hill behind our house. The table was set for ten people. It was covered with a beautiful white damask tablecloth and matching napkins. The china was white Limoges trimmed with a wide gold border. In front and to the right of each plate were four crystal glasses: one for water, one for white wine, one for red wine and one for dessert wine. The silver place settings were brightly polished. At every other place setting was a small crystal salt cellar and tiny serving spoon. Before the meal, the adults had an apéritif which was usually a glass of vermouth over ice with a lemon peel. It was a custom to gently trink the glasses and say, "A votre santé." ("To your health".) The first course was an antipasto which consisted of Genovese salami, hard boiled eggs, olives, thinly sliced ham, anchovies, sardines, artichoke hearts, and mushrooms which had been soaked in Italian salad dressing. The fish course was served next followed by some type of pasta or homemade ravioli. After that, there was the meat course served with fresh vegetables. The garden salad seasoned with Italian dressing was always served after the main course because it was refreshing. Next, a platter of various cheeses was brought to the table: Roquefort, Camembert, Brie and Goat. They are still my favorite cheeses. Of course, all of these courses were accompanied with French bread! The cheese course was followed by a bowl filled with a variety of fresh fruit. It is customary to eat fruit using a fork and knife. Cake was served next. Sometimes my aunt made special cupcakes covered with white vanilla icing and topped with maraschino cherries. The cupcakes were always stored on the card table of the sitting room and their aroma filled the room. It was difficult for me not to be tempted, but I waited patiently for dinner time.

At the end of the meal, everyone went to the living room for a musical interlude, to drink an espresso served in fuchsia 'demi-tasse' cups lined with gold and to sip a "pousse-café' liqueur such as Crème de Menthe, (mint), Cointreau or Benedictine. Before drinking everyone said, "A votre santé!" (To your health!). One might think that this meal was complete; but no, to finish it off we returned to the dining table where a huge basket of varied nuts, dried dates and dried figs was passed around. Everyone continued to eat while they talked and talked and talked.

The sitting room was so special to me because of the two stained glass windows decorated with blossoms of irises and butterflies. In the middle of the room was a square card table with drawers in which the cards and other games were stored. Against the wall on the right was a deep red velvet couch with two matching ottomans. The walls were decorated with pictures of the hunt and ivory hunting horns. My family spent many happy moments there with their friends. I especially liked to watch them play the French card game 'Nain Jaune' or the game of the Yellow Dwarf.

Next to my room was the marble staircase which led to the upper bedrooms. To the right, under the staircase was a cabinet against the wall. It was there that my Aunt Josephine stored her violin and mandolin. I often went there to pluck the mandolin. It was decorated with butterflies and flowers made out of mother of pearl. I hoped to learn to play it one day, unfortunately it was given away to someone else. After I was married and had two children I took guitar lessons. I used to practice the guitar in the woods by a lake while my daughter Michelle fished. It was her reward for bringing home good grades. Fishing is now one of her favorite activities which she shares with her children.

On the far wall of the hall next to an alcove was the door which led to the kitchen. Upon opened the door, you could see the double glass doors which were centered on the far wall. They led to a small porch and the patio. Under the porch was the house of our dog Fido. Dad told me, "When you were a baby, Fido took your entire arm in his mouth, but he didn't hurt you. He followed you wherever you went."

In front of the kitchen was a huge patio with four symmetrical circles. The two nearest the house were planted with persimmon trees, and the ones further from the house where planted with lemon trees. I always loved persimmons. They must be eaten when they are very ripe, because if they are not, they taste very bitter like alum. On the far left corner, were branches and foliage of the fig tree which was planted in the lower garden. The tree was too tall for us the pick the figs. My father's solution was to attach a metal funnel with sharp 'teeth' to a long pole. We had to reach the fig with the funnel, and then cut the stem with the sharp metal thus allowing the fig to fall into it. Until this day, I have a passion for fresh figs. On the left side of the garden was a balcony of concrete columns and in the middle were stairs leading to the lower garden.

In the kitchen were two built- in cabinets; above them was a window. In one cabinet there was a ceramic jar filled with black olives from our two olive trees which tasted like Kalamata olives. Occasionally, when no one was looking, I would grab a handful of olives. The kitchen was painted light green and the floor was covered with white and grey marble octagonal tiles. On the left wall on either side of the oak buffet were two built-in closets. One was used to store our everyday dishes and glasses; the other was used as a pantry. It was there that I always found my favorite sweet treat…gingerbread.

On either side of the door leading to the kitchen were two small oak tables. The first table had a large scale which weighed our food in kilograms. On the other one was our red iron coffee grinder. I enjoyed turning the handle to grind the aromatic coffee beans. Above it on the wall was a large oak pendulum clock. The stove, the oven, and the sink were lined up against the wall. Sometimes when the oven was not big enough for lasagna or

16

turkey, we carried our food to the local bakery to be cooked. Above the stove was a row of cabinets. In one was a bottle of cod liver oil which was given to me as a supplement. It was poured into a 'demi-tassel' spoon. Occasionally, I would take an extra teaspoon. I don't know why I liked it so much. In the middle of the room was a large oak table. We did not have a refrigerator, but we had a large pantry on the lower level with an ice chest.

Since we didn't have a refrigerator, food shopping was a daily task. We carried several leather shopping bags because the shopkeepers didn't provide any. They simply wrapped the fruits and vegetables with newspapers and the meat with brown paper. Every day we had to buy French bread because it didn't have any preservatives, the next day it could have been used as a baseball bat! When we went shopping, we had to buy each food from a specialty shop: the bread, rolls, and croissant from the boulangerie (bakery), the pastries from the patisserie (pastry shop), the meat from the boucherie (butcher shop), the pork and sausages from the charcuterie (delicatessen), the cheese, milk, and eggs from the crémerie (creamery), fish from the poissonerie (fish store), wine from the wine shop. Other products such as spaghetti, rice, olive oil, vinegar, salt, pepper, species, coffee, and tea from the épicerie (grocery store), fresh fruits, vegetables and sometimes fish were bought at the market.

I remember going to the bakery for bread. Everyone only bought the amount of bread they needed daily, so the bread had to be weighed. When we went to the creamery for milk we brought our own metal milk cans which were filled by ladling milk form the larger commercial milk can into ours. At the delicatessen, we bought sausage that we cooked with cabbage and served with a side of boiled potatoes. I loved the 'boudin' or black-pudding.

Because I spent a lot of time in the kitchen, I have a lot of memories. I used to sit at the table to play with my building blocks and my puzzles. My father built me a table with two benches which slid under the table. I set this table for my doll and me to have tea. Later my children sat at this table to color the pages of their coloring books. On day, I decided to set the kitchen table for the evening meal (le souper). The dishes were in the corner closet. The ironing board was parallel to the closet and the iron was plugged into the wall. In order to jump over the cord, I placed my right hand on the ironing board and the hot iron fell on my hand. Hearing me scream, everyone came to my rescue. A friend who was visiting said that the wound should be covered with a paste made out of cornstarch. Immediately after this emergency treatment, I was taken to the doctor. For weeks I wasn't able to use my right hand. I had to learn how to do everything with my left hand including writing. Although I still have a scar, it is not noticeable. Today, I always weed my garden with my left hand.

To this kitchen came a man who sold us Italian cheese. He placed the various types of cheeses on the kitchen table and with a corer he removed a small cylinder of cheese from the bottom side of each one so we could taste them. Each cheese had a special flavor: some were extra sharp, sharp or mild; some were dry or creamy; some were too salty. After we made our selection, he plugged up each cheese with the cylinder. From him we bought 'Toma', a cheese from the Piedmont region, 'Bel Paese', 'Parmigiano Reggiano' and others. We also bought French cheeses from the 'crémerie'. The French produce more than four hundred varieties of cheese. My goal was to taste as many different ones as possible; unfortunately, I became lactose intolerant. When I cheat, I pay to price; however, I'm not allergic to goat cheese which I love!

I spent many happy times in the kitchen. My father, who liked to tease, pushed my face into the whipped cream of my birthday cake! One Easter I received a special present. It was a toy chicken with real white feathers. My father said, "Appuye ta main sur le dos de la poule." ("Press your hand on the back of the chicken.") When I did, she laid chocolate eggs! I was so excited! I wish I still had it so I could show it to my grandchildren! I remember having to stand on a stool to hold the bowl for my Aunt Josephine as she made cakes from scratch.

Since we are in the kitchen, I would like to share with you some of our favorite recipes. We had a vegetable garden, so we had all the ingredients to make a Ratatouille.

RATATOUILLE

4 T of olive oil

1 medium-sized eggplant sliced 1/4 of inch thick

1 clove a garlic, sliced thin 3 small zucchini, sliced ¼ inch thick

1 cup of thinly sliced onions 4 medium-sized tomatoes, sliced ¼ thick

3 green peppers Salt and pepper to taste.

Four hours before, place the sliced eggplants in a pot, sprinkle each one with salt. Place a pan filled with water on top of the eggplants. Remove them from the pot and pat them dry.

Place the tomatoes in hot water. Peel them and remove the seeds.

Heat 3 tablespoons of the oil in a baking dish. Add the garlic and cook 1 minute. Layer the remaining vegetables and sprinkle them with salt, pepper, and 1 tablespoon of olive oil. Cover and cook on low heat for 40 minutes. If the vegetables are not tender, cook them for another 5-10 minutes longer.

The bouillabaisse is made with a broth in which there is saffron, garlic, fish, and shell fish caught in the Mediterranean. It is served with aioli made with mayonnaise and garlic. My husband and I had a delicious one in Marseille, France!

When I lived in France, I loved to eat the pizza made with chopped onions, black olives, (large and tasty like Greek olives), peppers and anchovies.

At home in Nice, I like to eat a sandwich with a sliced baguette sprinkled with olive oil and filled with sliced onions, garlic, black olives, sliced tomatoes and anchovies.

I loved the ravioli my grandmother made! We had a pasta machine to roll the dough into thin sheets. I liked to help her by turning the handle. The filling was made of different types of meat, spinach, eggs, and cheese. She placed a spoonful of filling on the bottom sheet of the dough, covered it with another sheet, and then used a ravioli cutter to separate them. They were placed to dry on clean towels which were sprinkled with flour. She would then put them in boiling salted water. When they rose to the top, she drained them in a colander. They were then transferred to a larger platter, covered with homemade tomato sauce and freshly grated parmesan cheese. I'll never forget when my neighbor in America and I decided to make raviolis from scratch on the hottest Fourth of July. She made the cheese raviolis and I followed my grandmother's recipe. We invited the neighbors next door and we still had raviolis left over. Now I use the filling to make manicottis.

1 roasted chicken white meat only

2 packages of frozen spinach cooked & drained

1 pound of sirloin roasted

1 can of liverwurst

6 slices of genoa salami

3T. of grated parmesan cheese

4 onions sautéed

Grind all of the ingredients except the eggs and cheese using a meat grinder. Stir in the eggs and cheese and fill the partly cooked manicotti. Cover the bottom of a roasting pan with tomato sauce. Place the filled manicotti on the sauce. Cover them with more sauce and sprinkle with parmesan cheese. Bake in a 350°F. oven until hot.

At Christmas, it was customary for us to visit as many churches as possible in order to see the mangers. The manger I remember most vividly was one where the manger was surrounded by mechanical farm animals. They were so amusing to watch. For Christmas, we usually made a Yule Log. How did this tradition begin in France? I don't know if what I read is true, but long ago a woodsman was supposed to bring a log to every family in the village so they could light it on Christmas Eve. When he realized that he didn't have a log for the last house he was supposed to visit, he went home and made a cake in the shape of a Yule log. On January 6, we always made a King's Cake. The cake was in the shape of a crown and a porcelain fève or bean was placed inside of it. The person who found the bean in his/her cake became the king or queen for the evening, received a crown, and had to select a king or queen. It was the custom for the recipient of the bean to invite all the guests to his/her house for another party. For Mardi Gras, my Aunt Josephine always made crêpes…very thin pancakes. I remember her putting rum in them and cooking them in a round fry pan. She would keep them warm in the oven until they were ready to serve. I make Crêpes Suzettes filled with a mixture of confectioner's sugar, butter and orange juice. The sauce is made with sugar, lemon peel, orange peel, orange juice, and butter. For New Year's Eve, I usually flame them with brandy and Curacao.

SUZETTE BUTTER

6 tbsp. butter

3 tbsp. orange juice or Curacao

6 tbsp. confectioners' sugar

Cream until butter is softened. Continue to cream while gradually adding sugar; set aside until oil is absorbed. (Butter should be soft.)

SUZETTE SAUCE

1 medium naval orange

4 large sized lumps of sugar

4 T or ½ stick unsalted butter

1 t lemon juice

¼ cup Cointreau or Curacao

¼ cup Grand Marnier or Benedictine

Wash orange and dry thoroughly. Rub the lumps of sugar over the skin and crush them. Transfer the crushed sugar into a heat-proof dish. Squeeze the juice of the orange. Add the butter, orange juice, and lemon to the sugar and mix well. Cook and sugar and butter have been melted and add liqueurs and heat to boiling point.

CREPE BATTER

2 tbsp. butter

1 tsp grated orange or lemon peel

1 cup flour

¼ cup of sugar

¼ tsp salt

3 eggs beaten

1 cup of milk

1 tsp Curacao

½ tsp of vanilla

Melt butter and set aside. Grate orange or lemon. In a bowl, sift flour, sugar, and salt. Beat together eggs and milk. Add melted butter, grated peel and vanilla. Add egg mixture to dry ingredients and beat until smooth. Heat a round, slightly buttered skillet. Pour just enough batter to thinly cover the bottom of the skillet. Transfer to a hot platter. Spread generously with Suzette butter and roll or fold in four.

In a skillet or chafing dish heat Suzette Sauce. When hot, flame mixture. Add crêpes a few at the time, until all have absorbed some of the sauce and are well heated.

In France, families also celebrate Saint's Days. Some children derive their name from the Saint's name on the calendar for the date of their birth; therefore, thy have only one day to celebrate. I was lucky because my Saint's Day didn't fall on my birthday, it fell on my Aunt Josephine's birthday on November 14. So I had two celebrations; however, for my Saint's Day I received one present.

On April fool's Day or 'Poisson d'Avril' everyone in my family tried to fool each other. I remember on one such occasion my grandmother got on the floor behind her bed holding a tread tied to a dollar bill. When someone tried to pick it up, she would pull the string! My father played this trick on me and on others. He showed me a nickel and he said he would place it on my forehead. Then he said to knock it down by tapping the side of my head. The nickel never fell, because he had already removed it. In elementary school, students would cut out paper fish with 'Poisson d'Avril' written on them. They tried to pin them on each other's backs without the person knowing.

Now I'm leaving the kitchen to describe the rest of the house. Next to the sink was a door which lead to a set of steps. At the bottom of the steps on the left was a door which led to the upper garden. Outside were flowers against the wall and a sidewalk leading to the back patio or the front porch against which was a garden of small palm trees. Going back to the house through the same door, there were stairs leading to the lower part of the house. The main hall was perpendicular to the stairs. We had a pantry room. In it was a 'garde-manger' or screened-in furniture where we kept perishable foods such as butter, cheese and milk under blocks of ice. Next to it was my dad's wine cellar. He bought cases of red and white grapes to make wine. He had wine barrels in which the wine fermenting process took place. When the wine was ready, he filled the wine bottles and corked them with a special machine that pushed the cork firmly into the bottles. The bottles were then placed on the wine racks of the wine cellars until they matured. To the right of the stairs was a half-bath. In the wall was a storage area for the coal that was brought in for our furnace. Going down the main hall was a room filled with shelves made out of wooden slats. It was there that we stored our fruits and vegetables. At the end of the hall were two deep grey tubs used for washing clothes. One of the tubs was used for washing; the other for rinsing. There was a scrub board in the sink and a pumice stone for removing stains.

On the other side of the hall was my dad's carpentry shop where he stored his tools. He had made a white outline of each tool on a board along the left wall. Around each outline, he strategically put in some nails so he could hang his tools. My father could do any kind of repairing including putting new soles on shoes. I enjoyed watching him and what he taught me helped me later in life. For instance, he taught me to put a piece of wood behind the "v" of the hammer to make it easy to pull out a nail. My son John is mechanically talented like his grandfather. When he was a child he would take his toys apart. When he was an adult, he took apart a large John Deer riding lawn mower in order to fix it. He placed all the parts of the lawn mower on the lawn and found that it had a defective part in the motor. He replaced it, and after putting the mower together, it worked great!

Adjacent to the coal burning furnace was the trunk room. Each of us had at least two trunks which we used when traveling. At the end of the hall on the left was the door that led to the apartment of our maid Margarita and her husband Guiseppi, our gardener. It consisted of a large bedroom with a full bath, and a kitchen with a dining area. All the windows were facing the lower garden. From the kitchen, there was a door leading to the garden.

To reach the second floor bedrooms, we had to climb the marbled stairs which were slippery. I had to hold on to the shiny brass banister; however, I remember falling once or twice when I was in a hurry. The first set of stairs reached the landing. Against the wall was a table for the telephone and above it was a window. The telephone was unique because attached to it was a hearing piece which allowed another person to listen to the conversation.

There were other stairs to climb before reaching the second floor. The hallway was perpendicular to it. Straight ahead were two bedrooms each having balconies with a view of the garden and the Mediterranean at a distance.

Aunt Josephine's room was on the left. Her dresser was on the right. On it she had a silver hair dressing set with a mirror, a brush and a comb. Between the two windows facing the garden was her roll- top desk. On the left wall was her armoire with carved columns on either side of the beveled mirrored door. Behind the door was her night stand, her brass bed, the sink and bidet.

The next room was my grandmother's and grandfather's. He passed away when I was three months old. After his death, my grandmother shared her room with my Aunt Jeannette who had returned home after her divorce. On the wall on the right was a tall bookcase with four doors covered with emerald green curtains. Inside this bookcase were marvelous books I loved to read, such as the Fables of La Fontaine, Lettres de Mon Moulin by Alphonse-Daudet, the short stories of Guy de Maupassant and Morceaux Choisis by A. de Lamartine. On top of this bookcase was my grandmother's bronze clock representing Henri IV holding his hat in his hand. When I was a teenager she gave it to me and it is still one of my treasured possessions. In the left corner by the French doors was a dresser. Nearby was a chair and a hassock covered with pieces of wool matching the rug which was designed with wine red roses. There was another window in the far corner. The right wall was almost completely covered by the huge armoire with four doors and beveled mirrors. It was tall enough to almost reach the ceiling. Past the armoire was a door leading to a large veranda. It was a pleasant place to sit and relax because of the view of the garden and the sea. Next to the window were the sink and bidet followed by twin wooden and brass beds separated by a nightstand with a white marble top. As a child when I got tired during the day, I loved to crawl into my grandmother's bed. I enjoyed feeling the cool fresh smelling sheets on my skin and soon I would fall asleep. It was in this room that my aunt Jeannette filed and polished my nails as I sat on the hassock.

I remember one day we all gathered into my grandmother's room to watch the boats coming in, because my father had gone fishing and suddenly there was a terrible wind storm. The furious wind or Mistral occurs principally in 'Provence'. The beaches of Nice are covered with 'galet' which are called shingles or coarse water worn stones. The wind is so powerful that the waves carry the shingles high in the air and they land across the boardwalk where the elegant hotels such as the

Negresco are located. That day one of my father's friends took a picture of my father looking up at these waves. When I saw the picture. I thought he was very brave to stand there.

Next to my half-sister's bedroom was a half bathroom. It overlooked the street below. From it we could hear the lady across the street practicing the piano. She was in her eighties and was determined to learn; therefore, she practiced several hours a day. Jeannine had her desk on the left wall. On the right was a night stand on which was a lamp with a green glass lampshade followed by a full-sized bed on which sat a beautiful doll with long blond hair. Her armoire was in front of her bed between the two windows which overlooked the patio in front of the kitchen. Her dresser was across from the desk.

Down the hall was the main bathroom. It had a tub, toilet, sink and a dressing table with a marble top on which were red baccarat bottles. There was a French door leading to a medium size balcony which overlooked the city.

The last bedroom was my father's. On the right wall was a night stand, a full-size bed, followed by a bidet and a sink. To the left of the bed was his dresser and across from it was his armoire, and a fireplace with a white and grey marble mantle. On it was his burgundy marble clock and two matching candle holders. His desk was on the corner next to the window.

Since childhood, I liked people and enjoyed being with them. I was thrilled when a family member would ask to go visiting with them. It was especially fun to go out with my grandmother, whom I called Mamina, because her friends made a fuss over me. My grandmother and I got along so well together. I loved her very much because she was patient and understanding. She taught me how to knit and hook. I was very proud of my accomplishments. In addition, she taught me many poems and songs which I learned by heart and recited to our friends. She even taught me an Italian poem: "La Farfalla Imprudente." I remember the story. There was a capricious butterfly that was flying from one flower to another and was never satisfied. In the end a little boy captured her with his net.

Most of the residents of Nice went to the country during the summer. Every year my family and I went to St. Bartolomeo, a small town in the Italian Alps. We rented a two-story house for the year. It was completely furnished. After breakfast, Mother and I took long walks in the woods. I ran after rabbits and butterflies, picked wild flowers, ate wild berries, and watched trout flowing downstream. In Italy, I had my first taste of Sabayon. It is a custard made with egg yolks, sugar and Marsala. We always made it using a 'bain-marie' pan or double boiler to prevent the eggs from curdling. First the eggs were whipped until frothy. The sugar was added to the eggs and whipped until the eggs became light yellow in color. The Marsala was whipped in last. It was not only delicious, but nutritious.

One day at our summer house, my father took me hunting. Fido our dog was walking on his right side; I was on his left. He told me, "Ne fais pas de bruit." ("Don't make any noise") so I walked on my tiptoes. The ground was covered with dead leaves which crackled under our feet. When we arrived home dad, hung the dead birds and squirrels on a rope. Someone took our picture showing my father and half-sister holding the rope, while Fido and I were sitting on the grass.

Jeannine and I liked to go in the woods to pick chestnuts and mushrooms. The chestnuts were covered with porcupine like stickers; therefore, we handled them as lightly as possible. When we picked the mushrooms, we had to be careful not to pick the poisoned ones. As soon as we arrived home, my father cut a cross on the flat side of the chestnuts which he roasted. Every time I smell roasted chestnuts, I remember those days.

One day at our summer house I was going upstairs to get a game and I fell down the stairs. My mother called the doctor who was a family friend. We called him Pillola (from the word pill). After examining me he said, "Rien de cassé, Marie. Elle a seulement été éfrayée." ("Nothing broken, Marie. She was just frightened.") Before he left, he gave me a banana to comfort me.

It was in Italy that I received my first fur piece. My grandmother had gone to Torino with my Aunt Josephine. When they came back home, I was already asleep but they awoke me and gave me an oval box with a painting of a blond girl with blue eyes and red cheeks on its cover. Inside, there was a snowy white fur piece. When I saw it, I was so delighted that I bounced up and down on my bed and said "C'est pour moi?" ("It's for me?") Then I kissed and hugged my grandmother and my aunt. I made such a commotion that the rest of the family came into the room. My grandmother put the fur piece around my neck and fastened it by shutting the mouth of the little animal on the middle of its tail. After admiring myself in the mirror, I was tucked into bed but before falling asleep, I pressed the fur upon my cheek. it was like a caress.

I started school at the age of six. Before entering, the school doctor gave me a thorough examination. When he injected the vaccine into my arm, I didn't cry because I watched him with interest. I was the only girl who brushed her teeth three times a day. My school, Ecole Saint-Maurice was surrounded by a wall. Every day in the courtyard before class the French girls and their teachers sang their National Anthem: "Allons enfants de la Patrie le jour de gloire est arrivé" Afterwards, we lined up and marched in silence up the stairs into the classroom. If we were not quiet, the teacher wouldn't let us into the room. Those who arrived late to class had to stand in the corner for the rest of the hour, if not more. When we didn't know our lessons the teacher hit us on the hands with her ruler or pulled our ears. Recess was held at 10:30. We played the same games that American children play: hide and seek, tag, hopscotch, ball and green light-red light.

Although we owned a vacuum cleaner, the woolen area rugs were often brought outside in the fresh air. They were hung on several clothes lines and were beaten with an "appetite en osier vernis", a carpet beater made of varnished wicker.

From the house we could hear the strange cry of a man yelling "vitrier" which means glass-maker. He was hunched over from the weight of the window panes he was carrying on his back. It was a struggle for him to climb the hill in front of our house as he yelled "Vitrier, vitrier, achetez vos vitres!" ("Glazier, glazier, buy your window-panes")

When my father had pneumonia he was treated with mustard plaster. It was a mixture of mustard seed powder, flour and water. The paste was wrapped in a piece of flannel and placed on his chest. The treatment apparently helped him to breathe better. Another time when he was ill, the doctor treated him with "ventouses" or suction cups. This treatment was used to promote circulation and to detoxify the body.

The adults of the family had a dressmaker come to the house to measure them for suits and dresses. They were able to select the patterns and the material. Many of the suits were made of wool.

We were living a wonderful live, but suddenly it came to an abrupt end.

Villa Trinchieri in Nice, France

My father Felix , step-sister Jeannine and Fido and I were sitting on the grass,
Post-War.

Father Felix (with a pipe) watching the waves caused by the "Mistral" wind.

WORLD WAR TWO

I shall never forget an encounter during the Second World War that I had with a German officer when I was seven years old. My entire family: my grandmother, my father, my mother, my half-sister, my two aunts, myself, and many other prisoners were traveling on a train from the Royallieu concentration camp in Compiègne to Vittel camp in north-eastern France. His kindness to me colored my feelings about the Germans for the remainder of my life.

In 1939, the world changed dramatically. We were forced to live through the chaos of six years of war. When I was three years old, I saw Mussolini in Torino, Italy making a speech to a large crowd. I thought that he was very tall; however, I found out later that he was speaking from a raised platform built for him. At that time he didn't think that the invasion of Poland would spread to Europe. Later, when he joined forces with Hitler, Europe was involved in a horrible conflict that eventually engulfed the entire world. My world was never the same after World War II was declared.

When the conflict was about to break out, we were on vacation in Italy. We chose not to stay in the Piedmont countryside where our family summer home was located. Because we held American passports, we left because we knew the danger of remaining in a country at war.

My view of war was different from that of my parents. In this time of high stress, my interest was focused on play. On the car trip from St. Bartoloméo to Nice, one of my favorite and earliest memories in those long-ago times was when I was sitting on the back seat of the Buick playing with my six three-inch dolls. My father had made furniture for them: six minute wooden chairs, a table and a bed. As I sat there, I "fed" my dolls and put them to bed covering them with a light green blanket. I still have five of those dolls and I cherish them and their furniture. I felt so secure on that trip, but our life was about to change dramatically. Although we had a chance to come home to America, my family decided to remain in France because of the investment they had made when they built an apartment building with sixteen apartments. The rent was our source of income and we chose to stay and protect our property. It was a decision that resulted in horrible consequences. My parents also feared that the ship taking us to America could be bombed and we would all be killed. They had heard that several families lost all of their possessions.

Then the war came to the Villa Trinchieri. I was terrified to see and hear planes passing over our house knowing they were going to bomb the city in which we lived. Did you ever see or hear planes passing over your house praying that they were not going to bomb the city in which you lived, or that at any time your house might be destroyed? I did, many times. When we went down into the cellar for protection, we had to wear hard hats and carry picks and shovels to dig our way out, if we were still alive. One evening, the sirens rang while we were having supper. We all went down to Margarita's apartment because it was more comfortable. My mother carried my bowl of chicken soup. She placed it on top of the sewing machine but because I was so short, I could hardly reach the bowl. The nights were very long when I was counting planes. Who would have known that twenty–five years later I would still be frightened by the sound of the planes flying overhead? One evening, I was in the kitchen of our home in Dover, Delaware preparing dinner for my husband and me when I heard this plane flying over our house. The sound was so loud that I thought the plane was going to hit the house. Suddenly, without thinking I threw myself to the floor. Years later, after we moved to our current home, I had recurrent dreams of fighter planes shooting at each other in the sky above our house. Brown children were falling from the planes on to the concrete patio. It was a terrifying sight. Another strange dream I had was the sight of New York skyscrapers crumbling as if there had been an earthquake.

On June 25, 1940, the Italian army occupied South Eastern France. Menton was annexed to Italy on June 25, 1940. In November 1942 "the Italian forces took control of Toulon and all of Provence up to the Rhône river, with the island of Corsica." (Wikipedia) Nice was also occupied.

In 1943, three Italian soldiers came to Villa Trinchieri to arrest us as prisoners of war. They gave us the names of several towns where we could live under their supervision. My father said, "We should go to Brides-les-Bains." "Why?" asked my mother. My father answered, "It's a small village nestled in the French Alps where there are many farms and orchards." My mother answered, "That's true, we will be able to buy food from the farmers." The village was chosen because of the many farms and orchards.

Before leaving the villa, we invited a French family to live there. An empty house would have been taken over by soldiers and would possibly have been trashed. We stored all the valuable antiques in the trunk room and wrapped them inside our woolen rugs.

The family brought enough money so we could live comfortably. In Brides-les Bains, we rented a chalet and were able to bring the items we needed for survival: sheets, blankets, pillows, kitchen utensils, dishes, clothing and personal items. Two weeks after our arrival, I was in the kitchen with my mother who was cooking broth made with onions for my grandmother who had double pneumonia when someone pounded on our door and said: "Offen sie die Türe!" Upon opening the door, we were confronted by German soldiers. They ordered us to pack some clothing in a small suitcase and be ready in 15 minutes to go with them. I was so scared that I clung to my mother's apron as she was packing clothes for me. "Est-ce que Mamina (our name for our grandmother) was mourir?" ("Is Mamina going to die?") She answered, "Non, ma chérie. Ne pleure pas." ("No, dear, don't cry.") The soldiers kept watching our every move. As soon as we were packed, they led us to a cattle truck which was already crowded with prisoners. After we climbed into the truck, they closed the door leaving us in darkness. It was very hard to breathe and some of the people fainted.

We had no idea where we were going. According to Wikipedia there were eleven camps available during the German occupation:

Fort des Ayvelle — a Nazi run camp from which Jews were transported to Auschwitz.

Baume-la-Rolande Internment Camp — a French run Nazi transit camp from which 18,000 Jews were sent to Auschwitz.

Camp de Rivesaltes — from which 21,251 Jews were sent to Auschwitz.

Camp des Milles — from which 2,000 Jews were sent to Auschwitz.

Royallieu-Compiègne — from which 40,000 people were sent to Auschwitz.

Drancy Internment Camp — from which 67,00 French, Polish and German Jews were sent to death camps.

Fort de Romainville — was a Nazi prison and transit camp, from which 3,900 women and 3,100 men were deported to Auschwitz, Ravensbrück, Buchenwald and Dachau concentration camps.

Gurs — was an internment camp for Jews.

Pithiviers Internment Camp — from which adults were sent to Auschwitz and the children were left behind.

Fort de Queuleu — was a detention center for members of the French Resistance.

Camp Vernet — 40,000 persons of 58 nationalities were interned in the camp.

The first stop was a school yard. In France, many of the schools are gated and surrounded by tall walls. We had to stand in front of a wall; everyone thought the worse, because the Germans were carrying machine guns and bayonets which they were pointing at us. Fortunately, it was only their way of segregating the elderly and the children from the crowd in order to give them something to eat. As an adult, I never understood why I felt uncomfortable while sitting at the dinner table with a knife or any sharp object pointing in my direction. Every time this happened, I felt a need to turn it away not knowing why. I now understand now that the sharp objects pointing at me where the bayonets.

We arrived at Compiègne a town 50 miles north of Paris. This camp was first used to house the French army and during World War 1, it was a hospital. When the Germans took over the camp Royallieu, they called it Front-Stalag 122. In 1941, after the invasion of the Soviet Union, Russians were interned there. Royallieu was one of the biggest transit camps in France from which 45,000 people passed through it between 1942-1944 (Delaporte).

On February 23, 2008, the interment and deportation memorial of Royallieu Camp in Compiègne opened. It was an ensemble of crudely built military barracks surrounded by roll after roll of barbed wire fence sandwiched between tall fences. At each corner of the camps were spotlights and lookout towers from which the guards made sure that nobody escaped. There were two dogs to guard us: a German Shepherds named Klopo and a Bull Dog named Prado. The women's barracks were separated and flanked on either side by the men's and soldiers' barracks. The soldiers who were prisoners of war were so thin you could see their ribs. They reminded me of the skeletons we hang on Halloween! We had no contact with the Jewish prisoners, because they were not near our barrack. In the article "Holocaust Education and Archive Research Team the Destruction of Jews of France", I read that 97 detainees died from malnutrition and disease. Before entering the barracks, all the prisoners had to line up to have their pictures taken. Each of us was given an ID which we wore around our neck. My family and I shared a room with about 20 other women and one child. They all looked like they were suffering from malnutrition. Inside the barracks were two rows of straw mattresses, coffin-like closets next to each "bed" and a black pot-bellied stove in the middle of the room. Because the mattresses might have been harboring lice, fleas, or other pests, we were made to shower with lye soap.

There were several memorable incidents that I can recall. For the first two weeks, our diet consisted of tea three times a day, boiled rutabagas and a piece of dried toast. The kitchen was in the men's camp, my father took the job of bringing us tea. Therefore, we were united for a couple of minutes each day. My father and other male prisoners discovered that our Red Cross boxes had been stolen and sold on the black market. Thanks to my dad and his friends, we were able to have food. Unfortunately, my dad and the prisoners who helped him were taken away and we didn't learn what happened to them for several months. After that, the Red-Cross boxes were given to us once a week. We had real food: evaporated milk, lunch biscuit (hart-tack}, cheese, instant cocoa, a can of sardines, butter, corned beef, sweet chocolate, granulated sugar, powdered orange concentrate, prunes, instant coffee, cigarettes, and tobacco. It was a blessing!

One morning, we were awakened by a blood curdling scream. "Qu'est-ce qui se passe?" ("What is going on?") One of the ladies who always wore her hair in a French knot woke up finding a mouse nesting there.

The water closet was outside. At night, it was especially frightening to use the facility because someone from the tower would holler, "Halt or I'll shoot" while the German Shepherds were barking ferociously. The spotlight on the tower beamed on us and we were asked to identify ourselves. My half- sister Jeannine said, "j'ai trop peur. Je refuse d'aller à la toilette quand il fait nuit!" ("I'm too frightened. I refuse to use the toilet at night!") Since I was a child, I sometimes had to go in the middle of the night; however, my mother accompanied me and I wasn't scared.

Because we were unable to bring a lot of clothes, our underwear began to fray. My Aunt Josephine tore material from the sheets and hemmed them again. With this cloth, she made us new underwear. She was very intelligent and tried to learn German so she could communicate with the soldiers to find out what happened to our father. Her persistency paid off in the end.

I remember three other prisoners. The first person was a little girl who was mean to me. One day as we were walking back to the barracks, she dug her nails in my hand and caused it to bleed. The second person was a gypsy who stood on her bed as she sang, danced and played the tambourine. Just before we left for the next camp, she gave the tambourine to me and it still is one of my treasured possessions. The third person was a French lady who was married to an American officer. She was hiding her diamond rings in her mattress. My Aunt Josephine said to her, "Vous ne devriez pas cacher vos bagues dans le matelas parce que de temps en temps les Allemands viennent les changer par surprise." ("You shouldn't hide your rings in the mattress, because occasionally the Germans come to change them unannounced.") Since the Germans sometimes made an inspection tour at night, some women piled a few pots and pans in front of the door so we could hear them coming.

After a period of six months in Compiègne, we were moved to Vittel a town in northeast France 165 miles away. It was known for the thermal baths, bottled spring water and lovely

42

hotels. We traveled by train. Inside the train, it was dark and it was cold. A German officer who was sitting next to me said, "Jemand soll dem kleinen Mädchen eine decke und eine heisse Schololade bringen!" He asked a soldier to bring me a blanket and hot chocolate. The fact that he did this for me inspired me to write this poem.

REMEMBERING

I have lived my life remembering
That black train in which we were traveling
All, prisoners, of the second World War
It was dark, frightening and it was cold.

I have lived my whole life remembering
A German officer who was so caring
Who gave a blanket and hot-chocolate
To a little girl like me…he was gentle.

I have lived my whole life remembering
The many thoughts that he was sharing
The terrible war he was forced to fight
The daughter he loved with all of his might.
Although he is dead, I want him to know

Just as him, love I was able to show
To our exchange students from Germany
Now, our friends and part of our family.

***

Now, I know the horrors of the Holocaust. Then, however, as a seven-year-old child, I had no idea of the atrocities, in which this officer participated. I only knew a cup of hot chocolate. While we were in the concentration camp, we never saw any Jewish people, because they were segregated from us.

I learned a great lesson from the German officer: everyone in this world needs to be loved. Love is a great force that should bind people together.

I feel that if I can make peace with my "enemy," so can everyone else—because I know from hosting German exchange students that they are not proud of the atrocities committed by their forefathers.

While writing about my experience as a victim of war, my emotions overcame me. The war made such an impact on my life that even as an adult, I was reticent to watch such movies as *Schindler's List, Life is Beautiful* or to read the *Diary of Ann Frank*, but I forced myself and was overwhelmed. I finally did visit the Holocaust Museum in Washington D.C., because I strongly feel that one should forgive but not forget.

The Germans had taken over all of the hotels which they surrounded with barbed wire. They called the camp Front-Stalag 194. The prisoners were segregated by nationality or religious beliefs.

There were Americans, English and people of Jewish faith. The Americans received better treatment. In our hotel, my mother, half-sister and I were in one room and in an adjoining room were my grandmother and my two aunts. Each room had a bed, cot, closet and pot-belied store. The Germans provided us with wood and coal in exchange for cigarettes which were included in the square Red Cross boxes. We were allowed to go downstairs to prepare our food in the hotel kitchen. It wasn't a bad life for me who was seven years old, but it was terrible for my family who didn't know what was going to become of us. My half-sister Jeannine was in her early 20's cried herself to sleep. I asked her, "Pourquoi est-ce que tu pleures?" ("Why are you crying?") She said, "Mes amis me manquent et j'ai peur que je ne les verrais plus." ("I miss my friends and I'm afraid I wouldn't see them again.") I tapped her on the shoulder and said, "Tout s'arrangera!" ("Everything will be O.K.!")

One of the hotels was transformed into a hospital and another into a school for us youngsters. There was a boy's school and a girl's school. Our teachers were Catholic sisters who were also prisoners. I learned from one of the prisoners that seven of the sisters were Americans from North Dakota. They were living in Brooms, France to further their religious education. The Germans came to get them on June 23, 1940. They traveled to Vittel in a third-class coach carrying ammunition. On February 29, 1944, they were released to be exchanged to liberate German prisoners in the United States. They taught us reading, writing, and arithmetic. The books were provided by the Red Cross. Many of us ate lunch at school and some of us helped prepare the food. I was given the task of cutting the meat in squares to make stew. One of the nuns thought I was too aggressive with the knife so she made me set the tables instead. Some of us who were old enough to receive our First Communion studied the catechism. The nuns also taught us many songs, and we learned new games which we played together during recess.

Every Sunday, my grandmother and I attended mass at a chapel which could seat 1,000 worshipers. The rest of the family attended the earlier mass. Because there was barbed wire around every hotel, the guard had to open the gate to let us through. After church, my grandmother and I took a walk around the park. I used to love to watch the swans bathe themselves in the little lake. When the sun shone, the ripples sparkled like stars.

For Christmas we gave our mothers a little gift which we had made ourselves during class. The Sisters surprised us with a Christmas party. Santa Claus, who had velvety red cheeks and smiling eyes, gave each of us a present. I received a puzzle and a pair of warm woolen socks. That day, we ate sweet fluffy cakes for dessert. We each were given a box full of cakes for our families. I was so happy that I ran all the way to the hotel. When I arrived, my mother had another surprise for me; a group of amateurs had practiced their acting and were going to perform the play "Sleeping Beauty" for all the prisoners at the town theater. The gray mice charades made an impression on me as they scurried around the stage. On a table were coats, gloves, scarves and hats of various colors and sizes. My mother asked me, "Quelle couleur de manteau préfères-tu?" ("What color coat do you prefer?") I immediately said, "le manteau rouge." ("the red coat.") I was lucky …it fit me perfectly. For a moment we forgot all of our troubles; after all, Christmas comes only once a year and why not be merry! However, our happy mood quickly changed because we all began thinking about our father.

When I told my teacher Sister Charles Amiée that we were going to be liberated, she gave me a beautiful card showing two children on their knees praying to two angels. On the back of the card she wrote: God Bless you! Before leaving the camp in February of 1944, we received a letter from our father telling us that he was interned in Clermont sur Oise. We wrote to him to tell him that we were liberated and that we were going back to Brides-les-Bains because all of the bridges and railroads leading to our villa in Nice had been bombed; therefore, it was impossible to go home to our Villa in Nice.

Our trip to Brides-les-Bains was very dangerous. First we took a train, then a bus. The trains in which we were traveling were being bombed, there was no place for us to sleep, and floods were numerous. The bus trip was very picturesque. When we approached the alpine region, I was so excited to see snow for the first time. The rolling landscape, the houses and trees which were covered with snow were sparkling in the sun. I exclaimed, "Que c'est beau!" ("How beautiful it is!") When we got off in front of the property where the chalet was located, we had to walk a great distance to reach it. I tried to follow the footsteps my family had made in the snow. At first, it was fun to run in the fluffy white snow, but when I arrived at the chalet my feet and legs were so cold that I began to cry. My mother asked, "Pourqoi est-ce-que tu pleures?" ("Why are you crying?") "Mes pieds et mes jambes me brulent." ("My feet and my legs are burning!") "Attends un moment", she answered. ("Wait a moment.") She came back with a pail of water. "Mets tes pieds dans l'eau." ("Put your feet in the water.") Which I did, and I soon felt better.

The chalet was as we left it; however, there was no heat. That night, we cuddle together covering ourselves with blankets and mattresses. The next day, while the adults went to find another place for us to live, Jeannine and I went sledding. She placed the sled on a steep hill and when I was comfortably seated in the back with my arms around her waist, she held the reins, placed her feet on the steering bars and away we went! As we slid down the hill the soft breeze mixed with snow blew on our faces and made them tingle. It was so much fun for both of us that Jeannine took me sledding two or three times a week!

My family found an apartment downtown. It was located over a grocery store. As we entered the apartment, the bathroom was on the left facing the hall. There was a living room, a kitchen, and several bedrooms. The apartment was heated with pot-bellied stoves. In order to have fuel for the stoves, we went and picked dead branches in the forest. We cut the wood and stacked the logs in bathroom.

In the kitchen there was screened-in furniture with shelves where we kept our perishable food under ice. My favorite cheese was Roquefort. One day, my family surprised me with a piece of it which we kept cool in this furniture. I loved this cheese so much that I ate a little bit each day so it would last longer. We were able to rent a piano. My god-mother Jeannette started to teach me how to play. After she taught me the notes, I learned to play my first piece "Estudiantina" a Waltz written by Emile Waldteufel. Jeannette was very patient with me and had such a joyful personality that all my friends loved her.

In Brides-les-Bains, I attended a one room school house and made many new friends. On Saturdays, I spent time playing with my friend Colette. We amused ourselves in the snow and played with dolls. I taught Colette how to read and write and every time she did her lessons well, I gave her a small gift: a marble, a ball, or a pretty picture. It wasn't much, but she was happy and this experience was the beginning of my teaching career. One day, we played in an abandoned garden of a large old house. Later, we found out that German soldiers were meeting there. From the windows of our apartment we saw the Germans soldiers marching in the street. The inhabitants of Brides-les-Bains did not tolerate French citizens collaborating with the Germans. Those who did, were made to march down the main street in shame, with their heads shaven.

While we were living in the apartment, I continued to study catechism. On the fourth of June 1944, when I was eight years old, I received my First Communion. I wore a white dress with a white veil that was attached to a crown of small white roses that flowed over my long and springy English curls.

The day my father came home was the happiest moment of my life. "Papa! Papa!" I screamed. I hugged and kissed him and asked him millions of questions. He told us that he was imprisoned in a building which was built to house crazy people. The panes of glass were at least one inch thick. In order to pass the time, he entertained the other prisoners by pantomiming or telling jokes. "J'ai un petit cadeau pour toi, Charlotte." ("I have a little present for you, Charlotte.") He handed me a small rectangular box in which was a tiny pink violin. He also gave me a two-inch metal train with movable wheels. "Merci, papa!" ("Thank you, daddy!") I sat on the floor to play with the train, but I was so upset when it was time to go to bed. My dad was my best friend; I never wanted him to leave me again.

POST WAR

෮

When the bridges had been repaired, we returned home to Nice. The family had taken great care of the house and property. Soon afterwards, we received a letter from the French lady who was married to an American officer. Because of this relationship, she remained interned longer than us. Since she was also a resident of Nice, we had the opportunity to visit her several times. She was a witness to the atrocities which befell the Jewish prisoners. Knowing that they were going to be led to the gas chambers, the Jewish prisoners were filled with anguish and despair. Some of the prisoners even chose to take their lives by jumping out of the hotel windows, thus ending their misery. She also told us that the seven nuns from North Dakota were released in exchange for several German prisoners of war in the United States.

My family made plans to return to the United States. At the time, no ships were available so we waited for almost a year. In the meantime, now that I was 9 years old I attended the neighborhood elementary school of Saint-Maurice. My father planted an extensive vegetable garden and we enjoyed eating the fruits from our many trees. For supper, I was often given a bowl of oatmeal with warm milk. I remember sitting in front of the bowl for hours refusing to eat. When friends came over they would say to me, "Charlotte, mange ta soupe." ("Charlotte, eat your soup.") The only way I ever ate oatmeal was when it was served in a soup bowl painted with an angel on the bottom. I knew that if I ate my soup I could see the angel; however, during the war my special bowl, along with some furniture were stolen from our house in Italy.

One day, a chicken appeared at our doorstep. Since nobody knew where it came from it became my chicken. Every day, I would go and pick a freshly laid egg. When we found out that a ship was leaving for the United States from Marseilles, my family quickly bought the tickets. It was fortunate for us, but unfortunate for the chicken, my grandmother cooked it for me and I ate the whole thing! Looking back, I don't know how I could have done that. I must have been really hungry! Our friends, the Deschamps, gave me a beautiful Limoges medallion backed with gold depicting Saint Anthony holding baby Jesus. This medallion is very special to me.

Nine Year Old Charlotte
in front of the U.S.
trimmed bush.

SAILING TO THE
UNITED STATES

On April 14, 1946, we left France on the Liberty ship S.S. William Whipple. Our trip lasted 16 days. On the way, there was a terrible storm. Since the waves were washing over the deck which connected the dining room and the state rooms, we had to hold on to a rope in order not to fall overboard. It was during this voyage that I celebrated my tenth birthday on April 26, 1946. The Captain had the most beautiful birthday cake made for me. It was round and decorated with pink roses and green leaves. The steward gave me a brown and tan balsam wood turtle whose legs and tail were attached by a wire. When there was a breeze, the turtle's legs and tail would move. I also received a jump rope from a member of the crew. He taught me how to jump rope very fast as if I were in training to be a boxer.

Between 1941-1941 two thousand Liberty Ships were built to move troops and supplies during the Second World War. Four of the Liberty Ships survived. The SS John W. Brown is located in Baltimore Harbor, Maryland and the SS Jeremiah O'Brien is located at Pier 45 in San Francisco, California. The SS Arthur M. Huddell was renamed Hellas Liberty. It is located in Piraeus, Greece. The SS Albert M. Boe was renamed Star of Kodiak and is located in Kodiak, Alaska. According to Wikipedia, I learned that Greek entrepreneurs bought 526 Liberty ships and Italians bought 98.

When we approached New York on April 30, 1952 we sighted the impressive Statue of Liberty with her right hand raised, and holding a burning torch, her left hand holding a tablet; she seemed to welcome us to America. I wrote the song The Statue of Liberty March in 1985 to express my feelings for this momentous moment.

(Verse 1)

Majestic Statue of Liberty

You light the

For people like me

Who seek to be

From tyranny.

(Refrain)

America means liberty

For you and for me…

America land of our dreams

That's where we want to be.

(Verse 2)

Eternal Statue of Liberty
Steadfast and true
We can count on you
For opportunity and equality.

(Refrain)
America means liberty
For you and for me...
America land of our dreams
That's where we want to be.

(Verse 3)
Enlightened Statue of Liberty
You show the world
That we live in peace
With every faith and race in unity.

(Refrain)
America means liberty
For you and for me...
America land of our dreams
That's where we want to be.

For some reason, the ship could not approach the pier so we had to climb into the small rescue boats. The little boats were bobbing up and down and side to side as they cut through the waives. For the first time, I knew what it was to be seasick.

When we landed, we were met by my Uncle Louis, my Aunt Philomina, and my cousin Marie. They drove us to Midvale, New Jersey. I had heard that behind their house there were mountains. When we arrived, I asked, "Où sont les montagnes?" ("Where are the mountains?") Having seen the Alps, I thought those were hills! My cousin showed me some of her toys. She had a toy kitchen with a stove, an oven, a refrigerator, dishes, a table, and chairs. I had never seen such beautiful toys before in my life, and I had fun playing with her.

My Uncle Louis had put a deposit on a house for us with three acres of property. The three vans of furniture from our villa arrived a year later. In the meantime, we borrowed some furniture. Not having much money at the time, we lived from the land. My father went hunting and fishing, planted a vegetable garden, and on the property there were grape harbors, apple trees, and a crabapple tree. The fruit is very bitter so we combined them with apples and made jam. We bought a cow and named her Daisy, not knowing that the lady across the street was also named Daisy. How embarrassing! The cow provided us with milk, cheese, and butter. I remember helping to make butter using a wooden churn. We also ordered baby chicks. They arrived by train and were in a box which had holes so they could breathe. Feeding them and giving them a drink of water was fun. We fed them mashed hard-boiled egg yolks mixed with corn meal. I was taught how to gently hold the chicks and tilt them a little so they could reach their food and drink. While I was feeding them, our English Setter Bruno was so jealous that he laid down with his nose in the corner of the wall! The chicks next diet was chicken feed which we bought in large burlap bags. My Aunt Josephine made dresses for me with the material of the bags. The dresses were pretty because they were of different colors and pretty flowers were printed on them. My Aunt decorated the neck and sleeves with rick-rack. I was so happy that none of my classmates made fun of me!

Some of the food we ate might seem strange. One dish I particularly liked was tripe soup. The thinly sliced tripe was cooked with red beans, tomatoes, onions, and olives. I liked it so much that I often had a second serving. My Aunt Josephine cut up the pheasants that my father hunted, browned the individual pieces, and cooked them slowly between layers of cabbage and onions. A delicious meal! My grandmother also made great gnocchis or potato dumplings. One day, my father and I tried to make them. We made the mistake of boiling the potatoes without the skin! Since the potatoes were too moist, it was impossible to make the gnocchis because we would have had to add too much flour! We also ate polenta topped with fried eggs and parmesan cheese. Other foods I enjoyed were: pigs' feet, brains, chicken liver, bone marrow on toast sprinkled with salt, snails and frog legs.

One day, when my Aunt Jeannette came back from the supermarket, she seemed very upset. It was out of character for her because she was always friendly and gracious. She said, "While I was shopping, several people were complaining that there weren't enough items on the shelves. Apparently they didn't know how it felt to be starving." For my aunt, there was an abundance of food.

A few weeks after our arrival, I attended the fifth grade of the Wanaque Borough Grammar School. I was asked to make a speech about my experiences in France during the war. The words came out, but with difficulty. I couldn't remember the English word for train station. All the girls were very good to me.

They said I was a regular chatterbox, but I didn't mind because the more I spoke, the quicker I learned English.

During my last year of grammar school, I caught the measles and the mumps. I was absent from school for 16 days. One day, while I was feeding the chickens, they started running in the field. I chased them back into their yard and I caught poison ivy on my legs and arms. The itching was so unbearable that I had to be covered with calamine lotion. That week I didn't go to school. I was graduated from elementary school on June 21, 1949 when I was thirteen.

It was a tradition to give me castor oil to drink when I was looking pale. The oil was warmed so it could be swallowed more easily. The taste was so awful that I was given a slice of lemon or a small amount of crème de mint to camouflage the taste. The last time I took castor oil was during the Korean War. I thought of those brave American soldiers risking their lives. I said to myself, "If they can put their lives in danger, I can drink this horrible castor oil" I forced myself to drink it fast. How ironic that I would marry Dr. Joseph J. Ward, who was a Sergeant in this war.

Soon after our furniture arrived, so did the money we had invested in France. My family bought a ten-room house at 619 Ringwood Avenue, Midvale where I lived until my marriage on April 22, 1967. The new house had plenty of room for all our furniture and antiques. Before we bought it, there was a butcher shop in the front part of the house.

After we were settled, we opened an ice cream parlor. On the left was a soda fountain in front of which were tall stools with red cushions. On the right were several square tables each surrounded by four red cushioned chairs. The showcase was straight ahead a few feet away from the back wall and next to it was a rectangular oak table with two chairs facing the door. That's where my grandmother and I often sat while she taught me poems in several languages and where my Aunt Josephine taught me to write the address straight on an envelope. It took a lot of practice!

At that time, the candy was called penny candy. My favorite chocolate candies were filled with vanilla cream, strawberry cream, or cherries. I could make my own ice cream soda. It consisted of $\frac{1}{4}$ cup of frozen strawberries with syrup, $\frac{3}{4}$ cup of strawberry ice cream, $\frac{3}{4}$ cup of cold cream soda, and topped with whipped cream and strawberry halves.

My mother and I were invited to spend the night at her sister's house in Paterson, New Jersey. I remember being asked what I wanted for breakfast. I was very surprised because when I was growing up, I always ate what was placed before me except for the oatmeal, of course!

My mother divorced my father, three years after returning to America. I had to go to court and the judge asked me if I wanted to live with my mother or my father. I chose to live with my father. Due to the traumatic experience I had when I was separated from him during the war and I didn't know if I would ever see him again. While growing up, my father and I were very close. He took me fishing, played games with me, made furniture for me and my dolls, listened to the radio with me and took me with him when he visited his friends.

One time, my dad took me fishing at night. We had to climb the mountain behind my uncle's house; it was so dark that I often wondered how he found his way. On the other side of the rise there was the Wanaque reservoir. It was there that I caught my first fish: a sunfish. I was so excited that I landed the fish in the pine tree behind me. Dad had to climb the tree to get the fish and had to untangle my line! It was a tradition for us to go trout fishing on the first day of the fishing season. We had to get up very early to get to his favorite spot. Father was great at catching fish because he could feel the fish biting on the bait. We always went home after catching our limit. One morning when we arrived to our spot a little late, we saw another man fishing there. The man said to my father, "I'm fishing in the same spot where you were yesterday, but I didn't catch any fish." My father replied, "Do you speak French?" The man responded, "No." "Then," my father added, "If you don't speak French, you'll not catch any fish because I speak French to them."

Father and I played card games together such as 21; One, Two, Three; and the Deep Blue Sea and Pinochle, but we never played for money. We played board games such as dominos, checkers and Chinese checkers. Sometimes we would play cards at one of the tables of the Ice-Cream Parlor with some of my classmates. Father taught me how to play Ping-Pong which is still my favorite sport. I learned to serve a wicked fast ball close to the net and also learned not to stand close to the table. After I started to play quite well, my father would make funny faces at me so I would get distracted.

He and I watched television at the home of the Jordan family in Wanaque. Sometimes Jeannine would come with us too. The shows were in black and white. We saw such programs as "Your Show of Shows" with Cid Caesar and Imogene Coca, "I Love Lucy," "The Lone Ranger," "Roy Rogers, "Lucy and Desi Comedy Hour," "Jackie Gleason," "The George Burns and Gracie Allen Show," "Amos and Andy," "The Red Skelton Show," and my two favorite shows "Lassie and the Adventures of Rin Tin Tin." At home, Jeannine and I listened to a soap opera in Italian on the radio. We also listened to the "The Shadow".

This was a very scary show for me, it was an evening show and afterwards I had to climb the stairs to my room and go to bed. In my room was the door leading to the attic. I imagined creepy sounds coming from the attic, and I had difficulty going to sleep.

My mother had visitation rights. The last time she came to visit me, she had tears in her eyes. I remember shaking all over because I was afraid that she was going to take me away from my dad. As you remember, when we were in concentration camp my dad was taken away. I never wanted to be separated from him again. I remained with my dad, my half-sister, and my two aunts who raised me. I often wondered why mother left. Perhaps, it was that in America she discovered a new life style and wanted to leave all those years of pain and suffering behind her.

When I gave birth to my son John, I understood for the first time what it was like to be a mother. My mother's tears had haunted me. After my dad passed away, I decided that I needed to look her up. It was not my intention to hurt anyone in my family, but it was just something I had to do. I remembered that her brother had a hardware store so I called there, talked to him, and asked him to contact my mother. That evening, I received a phone call from her husband Paul who told me that we could come and visit, but he wanted me to be careful to not hurt her feelings because she wasn't feeling well. When we arrived, we were greeted warmly. They made tea for us, had bought delicious Italian pastries, and had milk in the refrigerator for our son. It was a pleasant visit. My mother was very happy to see us and smiled a lot. My stepfather was very friendly, cheerful and kind, like my father. Coincidently, they were both born under the Gemini sign. We returned several times to visit them until the day my stepfather called to tell me that my mother had to be placed in a nursing home. She didn't remember him, didn't sleep well during the night, and he told me that it was better that I didn't visit her there. So I honored his request and never saw her again. At least she got to see us and her grandson, and for this I was grateful.

When I attended Butler High School, in Butler, New Jersey, I participated in the following extra-curricular activities: Choir, Glee Club, French Club, Future Teachers of America, Folk Dancing Club, and Poster Club. I enjoyed these clubs tremendously because each of them reminded me of the things I enjoyed when I was younger such as music, teaching and art. My family had been very strict with me. I could not go out at night and was never allowed to go to a school dance. When I went to my 35th class reunion with my husband, we sat by a classmate who knew my father. He told us that my dad had taught him how to hunt and fish. He also shared with me that my dad told him that while growing up, I was never allowed to do anything. It was true. I was overly protected, but I survived.

RETURN HOME

On September 11, 1951, my family and I returned to Nice to sell our properties. We sailed on the S.S. Independence. This ship was air conditioned. Our cabin had a private bathroom, telephone, and looked like a spacious living room by day. At night we were able to convert the sofas into comfortable beds. After breakfast, I joined the various tournaments such as ping-pong, shuffleboard, and horse-shoe. The contests lasted until 4 o'clock, but we took a break for lunch. I was always rushing! The movies began at 4:30 p.m. and lasted until dinner time. In the evening, I danced, played cards, played ping-pong, or just sat outside watching the beautiful multicolored sunsets.

Although it was September when we arrived in Naples, Italy the weather was just as warm as it is in New Jersey in July. Reflecting into the clear blue waters of the bay, the lovely white houses seemed to dance with joy. In the distance we could see the Vesuvius. On September 20, we arrived in Cannes. On the turquoise-blue water, sailboats were floating lazily along. The mountains, orchards, flowers, palm trees, and the ocean together made a breathtaking panorama.

When we arrived in Nice, our friends received us with open arms. We were invited for dinners here and teas there. Each day of the week was scheduled. I was enrolled at the Lycée de Jeunes Filles, a private girls' school. It was the same school that my half-sister attended. In order to be accepted, I had to take exams in French, Geometry and English. Everyday my friend Genevieve and I left our homes at 7:15 a.m. and walked to school to arrive in time for the eight o'clock classes. They kept standard time there. Just imagine how dark it was. Sometimes we even saw stars! It was the custom to return home for lunch and then go back to school until the 5:00 p.m. closing. We didn't have to go to school on Thursdays, Saturday afternoons or Sundays.

The lessons were very difficult. I always had lots of homework! My subjects were French, English, Italian, Algebra, Geometry, History, Geography, Science, Music, Art, Physical Education, Art History, and Sewing. We had to take notes, but the teachers spoke so fast it seemed that they did not take time to breathe! I learned many poems in French, English and Italian. One of the poems we studied in English is in the book "Tennyson's Idylls of the King." In sewing class we made stockings with four needles. We were required to make maps in Geography and History classes.

During recess, our class sold croissants to help defray the cost of a school outing that was planned to visit the country of Monaco. On September 29, 1951, with my new friends, I visited Monte Carlo, the Prince's Palace, the exotic gardens, and the underground caves in Monaco. We also visited the butterfly museum of Cap-Ferrat, the shrine of Our Lady of Laghet, and so many other places. School was not in session on Thursdays,

Saturday afternoons, or Sundays. In the evenings, Jeannine and I sat at the piano and sang all of the popular French songs. When our best friends visited, they brought violins and a cello. My sister accompanied them with the piano, while my Aunt Jeannette sang. It was the sweetest music this side of Heaven!

During the summer months, my sister Jeannine and I walked to the beach. I was taking swimming lessons in the Mediterranean Sea while she was sunbathing. The swimming instructor had each of his students put on a floating belt. He stood on the pier holding a fishing pole. At the end of the fishing line was a hook attached to the belt of the students. While I was waiting for my turn, I screamed "Regarde Jeannine, une femme est tombée dans l'eau!" (Look Jeannine, a woman fell in the water!) She was very heavy and her weight broke the line. The instructor jumped into the sea to rescue her. Later, he told my sister that he didn't like the water! We always stayed at the seashore until late morning. On the way home we shopped for fruits and vegetables which were displayed on long, wide tables along the sidewalk. At least once a week we also bought flowers. Carnations and mimosas were our favorite flowers.

Nice is a popular city for tourism, not only for its climate, but also for all of its many festivals. We attended numerous carnivals and flower battles during which the girls would stand on the floats while throwing flowers to the waiting crowd and some of the people threw them back. We also enjoyed going to see the fireworks, folklore parades, and religious feasts. The city is always crowded when there is a festival. I was walking with my dad on the way to the carnival when suddenly the people who surrounded us actually lifted me off my feet! Many carnival fans like to play jokes. One man asked my dad, "Quelle heure est-il?" ("What time is it?") While my dad was looking at his watch, the man took off my dad's hat, filled it with confetti and dumped it on his head.

Since the properties were not sold immediately, it was decided that my father, half- sister, and I would spend three weeks in Italy before returning to the United States. We revisited places I had seen when I was a little girl. In Italy we visited San Bartolomeo where we had our summer house. Our friends who knew me when I was a child were surprised to see how much I had grown! The last time I saw them I was six years old and now I was sixteen. The Italian doctor who came to see me when I had fallen down the stairs picked us up one evening in his Ferrari. My father was sitting in the front and my half-sister Jeannine and I were sitting in the back. He was smitten with my sister, and wanted to marry her, but she wasn't interested in him. While listening to the conversation I became very emotional and began to cry. I was hoping she would change her mind, because he was handsome and kind. In the end, she never married. After we left him, we continued our journey to visit Torino, Milano, Naples and Sorrento.

In March 1953 Dad, my half-sister Jeannine, and I returned home on the S.S. Independence. The trip was the same as the one going to Europe, except for the fact that I won two contests: the ping-pong and the horse-shoe competitions. I was given a green wallet with S.S. Independence inscribed on it and a photo album in which I placed all of the postal cards collected in France and in Italy.

When the three of us returned home, for the first time in my life I felt that I was living in a real family situation. A father at the helm and a half-sister with whom I felt I could get along without fighting. We worked side by side making dinner and cleaning up. She washed the dishes and I dried them. One night,

I felt like Cinderella when my dad allowed me to go to my first school dance.

After Easter vacation at the age of 17, I returned to Butler High School. During those last two years, I went on many of the school's field trips. Our trip to visit the United Nations was the most memorable one. We crowded into our chartered bus at 8 o'clock in the morning. When we arrived in New York the sun, which was shining brightly, gave us a warm welcome. The almost dim lighting and the glass panels of the main public entrance of the General Assembly building, which were set into lofty marble piers, made me feel the same protection, peace, and contentment that I experienced when walking into cathedrals. The sparkling white balconies leading to the public galleries were modern in design.

In groups of twenty, we promptly started the tour at 9:30 a.m. We ate lunch in one of the Delegates' private restaurants which overlooked the clear blue waters of the East-River. Imagine our surprise and delight when we were told that Mrs. Vijaya Lakshmi Pandit from India President of the United Nations General Assembly, had dined there just a while before. After we had eaten, we visited the Meditation Room. Its simplicity was calming. There, the delegates from all the corners of the earth come to pray. In that same room, we also prayed. We prayed for Peace. Peace for all the people of this world. While I prayed, peacefulness overcame me, a peacefulness like I never felt before. Our tour ended in the Public Concourse. In this area was the U.N. Bookshop, the U.N. Gift Center displaying colorful and representative items from many countries belonging to the U.N., and a Post Office, where some of us bought U.N. Stamps. On the way home, we sang our favorite songs and the monotonous rattle of the motor and rumble of the wheels were lost in the background.

In 1954, I was accepted to attend Montclair State Teachers College in Montclair, New Jersey. When I arrived I was actually surprised at the friendly atmosphere because I had heard rumors that the students there were stuck-up students. Every day, I commuted by train from Midvale to Upper Montclair. While in college, I thought about my future. My greatest desire was to become a French teacher. One day, I read "My Aim" by G.L. Banks. What he said expressed my feelings completely. He wrote the following:

> "I live for those who love me, for those who know me true;
>
> For the Heaven that smiles above me, and awaits my spirit too;
>
> For the cause that lacks assistance, for the wrong that needs resistance,
>
> For the future in the distance, and the good that I can do."

I earned a B.A. in French from Montclair State Teacher's College in 1958, I studied Spanish at Seton Hall University, earned my M.A. degree in foreign languages from Montclair State Teacher's College in 1970 and received a B.A. degree in Spanish from Delaware State College in 1979.

FAMILY AND EXTENDED FAMILY

As I look back at my life, I feel that I have accomplished my goals of having a successful career, getting married, and having children. I was a French and Spanish teacher for forty-two years. I was married at age 29 to Dr. Joseph J. Ward, a Chiropractic Physician, and we had two children: a son, John Charles , and an adopted daughter, Michelle Patricia.

As they were growing up we taught them to be respectful to people of different races and creeds. We taught them these values by participating in the following exchange programs: American Field Service, Youth for Understanding, the Belfast Project, the Foreign Study Tour, and Nacel Cultural Exchanges. We also hosted Fresh-Air children in addition to more than 40 exchange students, and teachers from around the world. Our students came from Belgium, Costa Rica, France, Ireland, Italy, Japan, Panama, Spain, and Turkey.

One of our exchange students, Bill from Costa Rica, came to live with in 1969 when he was sixteen years old. He was supposed to stay for three months, but he stayed nine years. It must have been my cooking! Even now, he calls me for one of my recipes. When he came to live with us in Dover, Delaware in November, he was 16 and could barely speak English. The next morning, he went outside to explore the area. He thought it was a beautiful day because the sun was shining, but it was freezing cold. The climate in the U.S. and in Costa Rica are in reverse. Even though I spoke Spanish, I always spoke to him in English using cognates, gestures and visuals. He attended Dover High School in Dover, Delaware where I taught French. In the evening, we spent hours deciphering the math book. He later became a math major in college! He applied to become an American citizen, and we went to Philadelphia, Pennsylvania where he took the Oath of Allegiance to the United States of America. Now he has a Master's degree in computer engineering. He and Tatiana, who is from Ecuador, have a son named Sebastian. They are a part of our family.

In February of 2006, the four of us went to Costa Rica for two weeks. We went to celebrate the 70th birthday of Maria Eugenia, Bill's mother. Her sons Louis, Bill (Guillermo), and Oscar dressed up in bright carnival-like papier-mâché costumes. Bill's costume represented the devil. All three danced with the guests. There was a karaoke machine and I sang "Eres-tu" with his uncle Mariano. Not only did they have a beautiful cake for their mother, but they also had one for me because I was turning 70 in April. I was so touched.

The next day, we rented a car to explore Costa Rica. In 2013 when my husband and I took a cruise of the Panama Canal, Bill's mother Maria Eugenia; his brother, Oscar; and Luis's wife,

Roxanne met us at the pier in Costa Rica. I was so excited to see them that I had tears in my eyes. Even though it was 100 degrees Fahrenheit, we were able to visit a church, an art gallery, an aquarium, and a zoo.

***

We are very close to Otto, an exchange student from Switzerland. He is married to Doris, and they have three sons: Philip, Sebastian, and Dominic. Philip came to stay with us for a couple of weeks. We went to Cape May, New Jersey by ferry, our son took him to Philadelphia and New York City. Otto was the mayor of his town and Doris was a teacher. They came to visit us twice. We visited them three times.

The first time we were there we visited his office and learned about their customs. We really enjoyed our trip to Engelburg where they have a chalet. While there, we visited Mount Titlis which has an altitude of 10,000 feet. We walked through an ice tunnel to a patio and from there we could see the skiers. Another day, they drove us through the mountains on the way to Lucerne. During this trip, we saw mountains in the background and villages reflecting in the clear blue lakes.

The second time we saw them was in July of 2012. We had flown to Stuttgard to attend Tobi's and Sarah's civil wedding in Tubigen. From there, we took a train to Zurich where Otto picked us up. It's always a pleasure to sit at the dinner table with them, their three sons and their girlfriends. The treated us to a boat ride on Lake Lucerne and we stopped at a little village for a picnic lunch. The highlight of the trip was the celebration of the anniversary of Dietikon, Switzerland.

In October of 2017, I flew to Zurich to spend a week with them. I went alone, because my husband Joseph passed away on December 14, 2016. We missed our 50th wedding anniversary by 4 months. They asked me what I wanted to see and I said the countryside. I love to take pictures, so this was a very great opportunity to see the beauty of their country. After a week's stay in Switzerland, Otto accompanied me to the Swiss part of Lago Magiori where Heiner and Ira picked me up. On the way to their home in northern Germany they dropped me off at Tobi's house. Otto and Doris are planning to visit me next year.

***

We became good friends with Marie-Jo a chaperone from Paris who usually visits us every year in August. She was teaching English to the hearing impaired. We always celebrate her birthday together. When she is here we play scrabble. Sometimes we play using two languages: one of us plays in French while the other one plays in English. While she is here we always spend a day at the beach in Rehoboth, Delaware and one day shopping at the outlets.

The advantage of living in Delaware is that we are so close to the major cities. That is why we were able to invite all of our exchange students to so many places. In 2014, since Marie-Jo had been to all of them, we decided to invite her to spend a week in Québec. When she was at our house she made a delicious ratatouille using the vegetables from our garden: eggplants, zucchini, peppers, onions, garlic and tomatoes.

Marie-Jo taught me how to make the best Chocolate Mousse for twelve people.

CHARLOTTE TRINCHIERI WARD

CHOCOLATE MOUSSE

5 packs of Baker's German sweet chocolate and twelve eggs.
Melt chocolate and stir in one egg yolk at the time. Beat the egg whites and add them to the chocolate without breaking the foam. Refrigerate over night.

We had the pleasure of visiting her twice in Paris. The first time, I was the leader of an exchange program and stayed at her house. Our group visited the beautiful buildings and Paris! I was in awe when I saw the stained glass windows of the Sainte-Chapelle. I felt that I was standing in the middle of a diamond! Marie-Jo was able to meet us for lunch. During our free time, Marie-Jo and I took a bus to see the flea market.

The second time we met her in Paris, we were with our friends Norman and Mary Ann. Marie-Jo took us by train to visit Claude Monet's gardens. I love Impressionist art and I was all excited to be standing with my husband on the Japanese Bridge! We also visited the Chartres Cathedral located west of Paris. It is a Gothic Cathedral which was never been damaged by war. When we went to Versailles, it was very crowded! We especially enjoyed the beautiful fountains and flower beds.

Our next adventure was our train ride to Nice, France where I was born. I had never slept on a train before where men and women were in the same quarters. I was happy that Marie-Jo came with us. I was able to show my friends the Villa Charles de Trinchieri, our former apartment building; however, I was sad to see that they had replaced our beautiful villa with a tall apartment building. When we visited the old city I said, "I need to buy a slice of my favorite pizza." Everyone chose the pizza they wanted. My toppings were onions, anchovies and olives. The flavors of the pizza brought me back to my childhood. When we visited the museum of Matisse, I heard a tour guide speaking in Italian. I was very surprised that I could understand everything he was saying.

On the way to Monaco, we stopped at the small village of Biot. There I bought a pendant made from a real rose! When we went to Monaco we noticed that the flag was flying. We were so excited, because it meant that the Palace was open to the public. After our lovely stay in Nice, Marie-Jo went back to Paris, and we started our guided tour of Provence, France.

We had a total of six exchange students from Germany. Tobi from Munich, Heiner from Dusseldorf, Clemens from Bonn, Frank, Michael and Ralph from Frankfort.

***

Tobi our exchange student from Munich, Germany was living a year with us and studied at Caesar Rodney High School in Camden, Delaware. Our children John and Michelle played in the band together. Tobi played the saxophone, John played the trombone and Michelle played the trumpet. While Tobi was here the entire family went to Disney World in Orlando, Florida. He returned to visit us three times.

The first time he came with his parents. It was amusing to hear him address us as mom and dad in front of his parents, but they understood. The second time, he rang the doorbell at around 3 o'clock in the morning. When my husband answered the door he saw a man with a mound of curly hair and earrings.

At first, my husband didn't recognize him. He had just come back from a humanitarian stay in Guatemala. He became a neurologist and also studied in Minnesota.

My husband and I visited them twice. The first time, Tobi's mother Elizabeth picked us up at the airport in Munich. Tobi took us to visit the Neuschwanstein Castle. While he was getting the tickets, we were struggling to climb the hill. Since we still hadn't joined him, he ran down the hill and said, "Are you alright?" Although I was breathing heavily, I answered, "Yes, we'll make it, don't worry." The castle was built for Ludwig II of Bavaria. Seeing the castle and the spectacular view was well worth the climb.

Another day, his mother Elizabeth took us to Munich by subway. Having traveled many times in a subway, I was surprised that the interior of this one was not covered with graffiti.

We stopped to see the Glockenspiel of the Town Hall, the Frauenkirche (Cathedral of Our Dear Lady), and the Nymphenburg Palace. Elizabeth told me that the Glockenspiel was erected in 1908.

I asked her, "How many times does it ring?"

She said, "Three times: at 11 a.m., 12 p.m. and 5 p.m."

"Who are the figures in the background?" I asked.

"They represent the Duke Wilheim V and his bride Renata of Lorraine."

There were two knights on horseback jousting.

"Who won," I asked?

"The knight from Bavaria, with the white and blue flag. The one with the red and white flag represents Lothringen."

When the music from the clock stopped playing, all the people clapped and cheered.

Before visiting the Cathedral of Our Dear Lady, Elizabeth pointed out the two towers to me. "See how high the towers are? The city cannot put up any buildings exceeding the height of these towers." We then visited the Nymphenburg Palace. It is a baroque castle where the rulers of Bavaria of the House of Wittelsbach resided. We were in the great hall.

I exclaimed, "Look at the beautiful fresco on the ceiling!"

"I like it too," she answered.

I asked, "Who is represented on the chariot?"

"It's Helios, god of the sun surrounded by other gods."

"Who was the artist? I asked.

She answered, "Johann Baptist Zimmerman."

We continued to visit the castle and I was smitten by the beauty of the Brussels tapestries! We ended our tour by walking the length of the grand parterre. On each side of the path were stunning statues of the gods of Olympus, beautiful flowers, and an immaculate lawn. As we were leaving she said,

"When the light is right the castle is reflected in the canal."

"It must be beautiful!", I exclaimed.

"Yes, it's too bad you didn't see it a night." "Would you like some lunch?"

"Yes, I'm a little bit hungry."

We sat at an outdoor table in front of the restaurant and ordered delicious veal sausage.

One evening, Elizabeth invited us to a German Beer Garden. She packed sandwiches in a basket. There were five of us: Elizabeth; her husband Anton, her son Tobi and us. When the waiter brought us the beer, he gave each of us an entire pitcher! I was dumfounded and said, "A pitcher of beer just for me! I can't possibly drink all of it!" We had a good time listening the band.

***

Heiner from Dusseldorf, Germany first came as an exchange student and returned five times in the summer. He loved the sun! He also brought books which he studied in preparation for his bachelor's degree. Later, he became a dentist. He married Ira, and they have two children: Julius and Greta. They vacation in the U.S. every year, and when they do, they stop to visit us for a couple of days. One time, Julius remained with us for two weeks and another year we picked up Greta at the Philadelphia airport for her two week stay. She was 14 years old. In order for her to come home with us we had to show our passports to the stewardess who was in charge of her. It was necessary to prove that we were the family with whom she would live.

My husband and I visited them several times. Each time they showed us different cities of Germany. The boat ride on the Rhine River was very relaxing! We enjoyed the landscape and the beautiful buildings. The day we went to Cologne, it was pouring rain however, we were able to visit the Cologne Cathedral. While we were there, someone started to play the organ. My husband who plays the organ said, "Can we stay a while?" We sat there in awe listening to the beautiful music!

We also visited The National Museum of Contemporary History in Bonn. As we were walking, Heiner said, "Look at the black Mercedes. It was Adenauer's car." (Konrad Hermann Joseph Adenauer was Chancellor of West Germany from 1944-1953.) Visiting the museum was like a walk in the past. Displayed were such things as an antique typewriter, televisions, vintage cars, motorcycles, tanks, uniforms, an ice cream counter and much more. What struck me most was a photo of Germans from Munich cheering in the streets when the American soldiers marched at the end of World War II.

In April of 2010, we met Heiner, his wife Ira, and their children Julius and Greta in Venice, Italy. The vaporetto stop was in front of our hotel and the hotel was only a five-minute walk to the cathedral of Saint Marco. We took a most romantic ride on a gondola which only cost $20 per person. The food was delicious! We discovered a lovely restaurant where the waiters wore tuxedos! We went shopping of course! I bought a red Murano necklace. To my surprise, my friend Marie-Jo had bought one just like mine!

From there, my husband and I took a train to Milan, Italy. We booked a tour of the city and got to see the Last Supper by Michelangelo. We were not allowed to take pictures. We also spent a day at Lake Como. It was at a restaurant in Milan that I tasted my first Limoncello, which is an cold after dinner liqueur. It is made with lemon zest, vodka, water, and sugar. It is delicious with vanilla ice-cream!

After three days in Milan, we joined Heiner and his family in Lake Maggiori. Breakfast and dinner were included in the price of the hotel. We had lunch in front of the lake, played ping-pong and swam in the pool situated on the roof! Julius went fishing in the lake and caught several fish!

Since Heiner had a car, we were invited to go to Switzerland. As we were walking, I spotted a jewelry store. I asked, "Can we go in? I would like to look at the watches." I ended up buying a Tissot watch! The next day, Heiner drove us to the Villa Taranto Botanical Garden in Lago Maggiore. The Scottish Captain Neil McEacham created the garden in 1931 and named it Villa Taranto in honor of his relative the Duke of Taranto. It is a magnificent 16-acre garden embellished by statues, fountains, waterfalls, ponds, and terraces. It is a haven for photographers! I took many pictures, but my favorite one depicted two Japanese cherry trees between which was a field of yellow tulips. In 2012 when we visited Heiner and Ira after Tobi and Sarah's wedding, they drove us to the Netherlands for a day and on the way back we passed through the French part of Belgium. In Bonn, they treated us to tea in the garden of the hotel where all the foreign dignitaries stayed when Bonn was the capital of Germany.

In July 27, 2014 Heiner, Ira and Greta came to visit us in Delaware on the way to California. The first day we visited Dover and the second day we spent at the beach in Cape Henlopen. On the way home Heiner said, "Let's stop in Lewis for ice-cream!" Everyone chimed in, yes!

When they visit, I must make blueberry muffins! Since I hadn't picked blueberries yet, Ira asked, "Can we all go pick blueberries with you?" Everyone was delighted when I said yes! In a short period of time we had picked 26 pounds!

The next morning, Greta asked, "Can you teach me to make the blueberry muffins?"

"Of course, it will be fun." I said.

Bill, from Costa Rica (an American citizen) and family joined us for brunch and all the muffins were devoured! In the afternoon Greta, Ira and I made chocolate chip cookies together. Greta loves them so much that I packed a bag of them for her trip. As always, they enjoyed our swimming pool and they loved Martini our English Terrier Pit Bull. One morning, we searched the entire house for Martini and we finally found her sleeping on Greta's bed! When they left, Martini wanted to get in the car with them. The children love the dog so much they have a picture of her hanging in their bedrooms in Germany. They don't have a dog, but they have two pet mice. They named them after us: Jack and Charlie!

In October of 2116 we met in the town of Lake Maggiori, Italy. While his wife Ira and I visited several islands on the lake, Heiner and my husband Joseph went to a five-star hotel to drink champagne and eat delicious appetizers. My husband really enjoyed himself and told his friends about it when he came home. One night, Heiner drove us to a fine Italian restaurant in the mountains. The roads where so steep and narrow that I felt dizzy. I had gnocchi (potato dumplings). They tasted just like those my grandmother used to make.

After a week In Lake Maggiori, my husband I went to visit Tobi and Sarah in Germany. We both were so happy to see their children: Xavier and Romy. My husband sat between them to watch children movies on their laptop, Tobi's mother, Elizabeth and father, Anton treated us to a bus tour of Regensburg. On the bus there was a radio that described all the important sights. We also visited the cathedral and took a walk to see the stone bridge across the Danube, which was built in the 12th century.

***

The third exchange student from Germany was Clements. He became a banker and worked at a German bank on Wall Street in New York. My son, John, and I were invited to stay with him for a week. He had a very cozy apartment with a living room overlooking the Hudson river, a closet for a kitchen, a bedroom, a bathroom and a loft. While Clements was at work, my son and I explored New York. We had a frightening moment while we were on the ferry on our way to visit the Statue of Liberty. There was a group of Japanese tourists with cameras in hand who all gathered on one side of the ferry to take pictures of the Statue. The ferry was tilting. I searched for the life jackets because I thought we were going to die!

***

The last exchange with German students was from a family of three boys: Frank, Michael and Ralph. Every summer we had a different son. After Ralph went back home, the mother sent us a letter saying that she had no more sons to send us...she could only send her dog!

***

Our son, John Charles Ward, was an exchange student in Canada where he went skiing, and traveled to Switzerland with us. He is married to Dr. Natascha Raminger. She is of German descent on her mother's side. Tobias came from Germany to be the best man for their wedding. Heiner, Ira and family also were there. At the rehearsal dinner three of the fourteen guests didn't speak German! During the celebration, Tobi read a letter of congratulations from Christian Wulff, President of the Republic of Germany from 2010-2012. It was a big surprise and was very much appreciated. In 2013, John also attended Tobias' and Sarah's church wedding in Germany.

Our daughter Michelle has four children: Bobby, Amanda, Matthew and Emily. We have four great-grandchildren: Riley, Brailynn and Levi (Amanda's children) and Audrianna (Bobby's child).

I tried to teach my children the same values that I taught my students: the importance of honesty, respect, trust, love and understanding for family, and getting an education. Without an education, I might still be wearing those dresses made out of chicken feed bags When you learn to love and understand your family, it is easier to understand your neighbors, the people in your community, and the citizens of other nations. I was inspired to write the following song for a student of mine whose parents were so active in the community that they didn't have time for their children. Their daughter came to me crying because she thought that her parents could not come to her graduation.

DEAR MOM AND DAD

Dear mom and dad
Please show your children
That you really care
By being always there.
Stop rushing around
And take the time
To look into their eyes

And listen with your heart.

Then all God's children (Refrain)
Will surely know
How to show love
And peace will come
To all the world
Because you were there
To show you cared.

Teach them respect
And understanding
So they'll learn to share
Their greatest thoughts and cares
Then they wouldn't need
To run away or go astray
Because you're always there.

Then all God's children (Refrain)
Will surely know
How to show love
And peace will come
To all the world
Because you were there
To show you cared.

Learn to get along
Find peace in your home
So the world will be
A better place for thee.
They'll be no need
For prisons or wars
Because you took the time
To teach them about love.

Then all God's children (Refrain)
Will surely know
How to show love
And peace will come
To all the world
Because you were there
To show you cared.

I hope and pray that I will see the day when people of all creeds and nations will hold hands and live in peace.

According to the source from two camps in which we were interned:

http://www.holocauschronicle.org/holocaustappendices.html

1. Compiègne-12,000 Jews were deported to Buchenwald and Dachau.

2. Vittel-300 Jews went to Drancy, 5,600.000 to 6,250,000 European Jews were executed.

The following are letters from two of my exchange students expressing their surprise when they found out that my family and I had been interned by Germans.

My dear American mom,

About 12 months ago, you told me that you were writing your memoirs. You asked me to contribute a letter about my experience as a German exchange student with a family of a concentration camp survivor. As a young girl, you and your entire family were captured during the second World War and held in a concentration camp by Germans. I thought about writing the letter many times but I always put it off. It is difficult to write about something so substantial, about a matter we have hardly ever talked about despite our close relationship, over the years and open conversations on many personal matters.

On a beautiful day of the summer of 1987, I arrived as a 16-year-old boy at your house in Delaware. Through the A.F.S. exchange program, I had some information and a letter from your family, but we had never met or ever talked before. Your husband, Joseph and your son, John had picked me up at the Greyhound bus station in Philadelphia. I remember you coming through the front door, when we pulled in the drive way of your house and my new home. You were smiling and welcoming me in your outgoing warm way. Then I met the rest of your family: your daughter Michelle and your "Costa Rican son" Bill. Everything was new to me, but everyone was kind and friendly.

The next day, you sat down with me and Dad for a talk and I remember your words as you said, "We know you have parents in Germany, but you can call us Mom and Dad if you wish." From that moment on, I was a member of your family. You treated me like your own children. You and my new brother, John and the rest of your family helped me select my classes for school, arranged everything for me to go to the homecoming dance, and brought me to school, for track training and band practice. You drove me to visit friends and had my friends over at your house. You made me clean my room, cut the lawn, and do the dishes after dinner-everything just like you did it with your own children. You had told me about the house in France where you had grown up a child and how you lived on the East Coast as a young woman and met Dad in New Jersey. You never told me why your family had moved to the U.S. and I never asked you about it. Around Christmastime, I had lived with your family for about four months—we were sitting around the dinner table having coffee after the meal, when your brother-in-law Tommy asked me about the Nazis. It wasn't long into the conversation, when you got up from the table and left the room. I didn't think your leaving the table was in context with our conversation. Dad turned to me with a soft voice and told me in two sentences that you were held in a concentration camp with your family as a young girl in France, that you were still often waking up at night having dreams about that time. He added that it would be better not to mention these topics in your presence as they would bring up horrible memories. At that moment, I was shocked. The stories I had heard from my German parents and grand-parents about that time, what we had learned in history class back in Germany, and the books we had read. In addition, I had seen the exhibitions in the memorial center of the former concentration camp in Dachau, near my hometown. It portrayed the victims as starving, suffering men, women and children with sad eyes. They were not portrayed as a kind, caring mother who smiled most of the time. It was my first contact with a victim of a concentration

90

camp; however, the victim was so different from what I had expected. In fact, the person I had met and lived with was not a victim at all, but a strong, successful woman, nurtured better than myself, cheerful, surrounded by family and friends and above all that she generously shared her wealth and happiness with me and many other people around her. I never felt sorrow, but amazement. I was amazed, because the Concentration Camps had always been portrayed to me as something final, desperate, and the survivors marked for life. Never had I thought that a girl surviving this experience would grow up to be a woman showing no anger, bitterness, or vengeance. After dinner that night, you and nobody in the house talked about it again and neither did I mention it afterwards. My year as an exchange student at your house continued, we got along well and as you mentioned several times since then, we never had any arguments or disagreements. From these times spent at you house arose some of my dearest memories of my teenage years.

The event at that family dinner; however, marked my heart consequently leaving a deep impression on my teenage mind. Thus, when I complained to my German family today about writing this letter that you requested describing an aspect of the relationship between you and me that remained unmentioned during all these years, they recalled that after my return to Germany my uttering the imprisonment of my host mother as a child by Germans. They remembered my amazement of the former iniquitous victim of our nation that took me in her house like one of her own children, never mentioning the past, not as a sign of forgiveness as there was no blame, but to experience a new culture, new home and family, and to enjoy life with a new set of friends in a different country, to which she had moved with her family after taking refuge from her home country occupied by Germans.

My amazement was carried over to my parents, brothers and sister, particularly when they met you at a visit in your hospitable house in Dover. This feeling was augmented by your obvious love for Europe when we saw your joy and interest about our country on your visit to our house in Munich. On our meetings, at many occasions over more than twenty-eight years now, at different locations in the U.S. or in Europe with different groups of people, it was always this joy and interest which you conveyed to everyone, never the memory of the history of your childhood with my people which always remained unspoken. Thinking back, I am grateful for this experience. I mention it often, when German history is discussed. Together: generosity, joy of life, and love of people are a tremendous force which conquers scars of history.

Love, Tobi

***

Dear Charlotte,

In the summer of the early eighties, I was for several times a guest at the home of the family Ward in Dover, Delaware. The first visit was organized by FST (Foreign Study Tours). I was an 18-year-old high school student. Dr. and Mrs. Ward had two children, a boy John and a girl Michelle. They all welcomed me heartily in a very interesting way. My "guest mother," Charlotte Ward took care of me and showed me "the new world." She really treated me as a part of her family. From the first day, I felt as if I were at home. Everything was new, very interesting and so exciting. The uncomplicated family life of the Wards helped me not to be homesick, but to be happy.

Charlotte Ward was a teacher; therefore, since it was Summer she was able to spend a lot of time with me. She treated me no differently than she did her own children. I was surprised by her open-mindedness towards foreigners, her heartily and lovely character and how she took everything so easy. I wondered, did she have bad times in the past that made her take everything so easy? She had no prejudices towards foreigners, colored people, handicapped people and not against Germans. She had a very, very big heart!

Of course, I thought about the reason for her immigration from Southern France, her native country, during or after World War II. However, I never knew that she had been in a German concentration camp.

Many years later after my first stay in Dover, we have never lost contact. When I heard about her "story" I was so surprised! I knew that she had a couple of German and Swiss friends, good friends with whom she kept in touch for many years. They all must have loved her. As for her, I can acknowledge that she shows no differences to her friends all over the world, regardless of whether they are from France, Japan, Spain…or Germany. I'm so glad that Charlotte could forget her bad experiences during World War II and be the person she always was: a cordial, loving and open-minded person! I have kept in touch with her family and I am still a part of her today.

Love, Heiner

Dr. Joseph &
Charlotte Ward
April 22, 1966

Tuesday, July 28, 1992   Section D

EDUCATION	TELEVISION	MOVIES	COMICS

A one-woman commitment to international good will

The U.N. in Dover

By NANCY E. LYNCH
Special to The News Journal

DOVER — Hosting foreign students filled Charlotte Ward's need for more family 18 years ago.

In no time, she adopted hosting as a way of life and today Ward's vast international family circles the globe.

"Our son, John, was 3 and an only child when we first started and we've been hosting ever since," says Ward, who is "Mom" to more than 40 exchange students from 10 countries.

"We've never had a bad experience," adds the soft-spoken Dover High School French teacher who's welcomed students since 1974 from at least six organizations, including American Field Service and Nacel Cultural Exchanges.

Some of her first students now have families almost old enough to be second generation exchange students. Ward knows because she stays in touch with nearly all her extended family.

"We've had so many returnees. . . Two brothers from Switzerland each came separately four times. The last time they came with their wives," says Ward.

Students also have traveled from Germany, France, Belgium, Ireland, Spain, Turkey, Panama and Japan to live in the Wards' modest home at 94 Meadow Glen Drive.

And two parents also have visited.

"The most students we've ever hosted at one time is three, but we have a 23-foot camper out back we use if we need it," she says. "And two students have stayed with us for an entire year."

Food is never a problem.

"We've never really thought about the cost. I can cook for an army," Ward says with confidence born of experience.

So strong is her family's belief in international diplomacy, she and her husband, Dover chiropractor Joseph J. Ward, invited last summer's exchange student, Javier Segura of Madrid, Spain, to return as a 1992-93 Caesar Rodney High School student.

Although the Wards have no exchange students so far this summer, they are hosting an adult chaperon from Spain. And Charlotte leaves today to chaperon a group to France.

As the Delaware area coordinator for Nacel Cultural Exchanges, Ward is always looking for host families for foreign youth. This summer is no exception.

Nacel, dedicated to promoting international understanding and language education through its home-stay program, provides health and liability insurance for its teen travelers.

Families interested in hosting should contact Ward.

"The love that we have felt from these students, the exchange of ideas and knowing that we're really all the same is the satisfaction of hosting," said Ward,

who points to her own background as an example.

"I'll never forget the German officer on the way to the concentration camp," recalled Ward, born of American parents in Nice, France. "I was about 7 when World War II came. We were in Italy and the Italians took us in first. Then we rented a chalet in France. The Germans came and gave us 15 minutes."

On the train to Compiegne, the first of two concentration camps where she and her family were held, a German officer befriended her.

"He sat me on his lap and told me he had a little girl like me at home and how he didn't want to fight the war. Then he asked for a blanket and hot chocolate for me. From that moment on, I felt that everyone was the same, I mean really the same inside."

Despite the memories of concentration camps, Ward describes her relationship with a German boy, one of her earliest foreign students, as "wonderful."

"Of course he's grown now, but we still correspond. He always asks me to remember him as 'your old German friend.'"

And Ward always will remember him and all her foreign friends.

"I used to cry all night when they'd leave. Then I decided I didn't have to. We stay in touch. These kids will be with us forever."

EXCHANGE PROGRAMS

Here are youth foreign-exchange programs that are seeking hosts this year in Delaware and nearby areas, with contact information:

AFS Intercultural Programs; Connie Logothetis, work 239-2634, home, 478-4425.

American Institute for Foreign Study; George W. Ludlam, 834-2992; John F. Swahn, 792-3415; John Keppelman, 996-0781. Divisions include:
■ Academic Year in America (call Ludlam)
■ Au Pair in America, for live-in European child care. Call (800) 727-2437, Ext. 6129.

American International Student Exchange; Students from 31 countries. Call (800) 742-5464.

Aspect Foundation; Students from more than 20 countries. Call (800) 879-6884.

AYSE International; formerly American Scandinavian Student Exchange; Philip Alborn, Pennsville, N.J., (909) 678-7874; Leslie Boyd, Dover, 697-0592 headquarters, (800) 677-2773.

Bendall International Cultural Exchange; Summer or school-year exchange students. Call Steve and Melinda Robino, 322-8769.

Delaware-Panama Partners of the American (Delaware-Panama Partners Youth Committee), Delaware students can make summer exchange trip to Panama. Elcisa Tarzanin, 654-2631; or (215) 329-1394, Mike Polasz, 292-8734.

EF; A multiprogram exchange that includes two programs that sought hosts here, but either, call Barry Diehl, 737-4981, or main office in Cambridge, Mass., (617) 252-6161. The divisions are:
■ EF Foundation, working with Asian countries.
■ EF Foundation; year-long student exchanges.

Nacel Cultural Exchanges; French and Spanish exchange students. Charlotte Ward, 697-0853, Denise Birger, 856-0705.

Spanish Heritage Students from Spain and Mexico; Jessie and Pedro Consuegra, Dover, 678-8540, or call (800) 888-9040.

Youth Exchange Service; Melissa Fitzgerald, Newport Beach, Calif., (800) 848-2121.

The News Journal/GARY EMEIGH

Charlotte and Joseph Ward have been hosting exchange students for almost 20 years in their Dover home. They have scrapbooks filled with memories, and legions of friends worldwide. Some of her first students now have families almost old enough to be exchange students, too.

95

RETURNING TO ROYALLIEU

Oops! I thought I was finished, but a phone call to the Royallieu-Compiègne Internment Camp was a new chapter in my life! The reason I called was that I had seen pictures of the camp online and I wanted to get permission to include them I my book. As soon as I introduced myself to Mrs. Anne Bonamy director of the camp she recognized my name. I was dumbfounded! She informed me that an exposition of the forgotten Americans of Camp B of Royallieu was going to take place from October 24, 2014 until April 2016. She asked me if I could come and make a speech. After discussing it with my family, it was decided that I should go.

We continued to correspond by internet and she wrote, "How fortunate that the internet exists, to be able to communicate with you." She asked me to send her my address so I could receive an official invitation for the varnishing. She was elated to have found an American citizen who could represent the United States. I asked her if I could make the speech in

French and in English. I informed her that my speech would be in three parts: 1. Introduction of my American family. 2. What a little girl of seven remembered. 3. Leaving France to live in the United States and the poem "Remembering." I sent it to her so she could review it.

She wrote, "After reading your speech I noticed that you spent several months in Vittel. One of my friends, Danielle Dubinsky who was close to your age was also detained there with her family. She will be present at the event.

After reading my speech, she made a correction. When I wrote about the solders looking like the skeletons we hang up on Halloween were not soldiers, but Jewish men. I was horrified, because I knew that they would have been transported to the death chamber. I asked her to tell me which dignitaries would be present so I could acknowledge them before I make my speech. She sent me the following list:

- The American Ambassador
- The representatives of the association of Franco-American combatants
- The assistant-prefect of Compiègne
- The curator of the Franco-American museum of Blérancourt
- The French representative of the Florence Gould Foundation who made a substantial donation to the exposition
- The mayor of Compiègne
- The local press and television reporters

In the next e-mail, I asked her if I could bring my friends from France and Germany. She answered: "Of course you can bring your friends: that they are Germans is a very strong symbol of peace and of reconciliation."

As soon as I received the good news that I could bring my friends, I contacted them. I called Marie-Jo and said, "Marie-Jo, on October 24 I'm going to make a speech in Compiègne in honor of the forgotten Americans who were interned in Royallieu. I'm so excited. Can you come with me?"

She answered, "That's fantastic! What are your plans?"

"I want to arrive in Paris on the morning of the 22 and fly home on the 27."

"Let me see if I'm free?" Pause... "Yes, I can go with you." "What time are you arriving in Paris? "

"I'm arriving at 9:30 a.m.

"You can take the bus to my apartment."

"Yes, it's a good idea." "I have done it before." "What hotel in Paris do you recommend?"

"The Tim, it's close to my apartment."

"I'll check it out, can you stay at the hotel with me? That way we can take the train to Compiègne together."

"Yes, it's a good idea."

"I'll call Madame Bonamy (the director of the camp) to see if she could recommend a hotel in Compiègne. I'm going to and I'll let you know."

"O.K". she answered.

"Thank you for coming with me. I'm going to invite my German friends now."

"See you soon." She answered, "Thank you for inviting me."

I called Madame Bonamy and she recommended the hotel Campanille Compiègne. I could not wait to skype Heiner, and his wife Ira as I do every Sunday afternoon 2:30 p.m. I gave them all the information I had given Marie-Jo. After they discussed the possibility of coming to Compiègne with Ira he said, "We would not want to miss it. We will drive our camper."

"That's a long drive for you," I exclaimed.

"No, the camper is very comfortable. It has air conditioning, a stove, a refrigerator, an awning, and tables and chairs."

"I'm so happy that both of you are coming."

"What hotel are you staying at?" he asked.

"I'm staying at the hotel Campanille Compiègne. Marie-Jo, my friend from France is also coming. We are staying from the 23rd and returning to Paris on the 26th.

Heiner said, "We shall arrive at around two o'clock on the 23th."

"Thank you so much for coming. I'll Skype you next Sunday."

"Great, see you Sunday."

Tobi was also invited, but he was unable to come because he had a medical conference to attend.

After speaking to everybody, I researched the hotels in Paris in the vicinity of Marie-Jo's apartment. I selected the Hotel Pavillion Opéra because it was much cheaper since it was being remodeled. I booked a room with two beds for two nights for October 22 and 26.

When I arrived at the airport Charles de Gaule in Paris, I asked where I could catch a bus. I found them lined-up near the exit of the airport. I reached Marie-Jo's apartment around noon. We had lunch together and relaxed. Around 4 o'clock we walked to her favorite restaurant near the Seine river. We returned to her apartment to get our luggage and walked to the hotel. The next morning, we ate breakfast at the hotel before taking a taxi to the train station. There, a kind lady helped me carry my suitcase down the steps. We bought round trip tickets to Compiègne which is located 50 miles north of Paris.

When we arrived at Compiègne, we took a taxi to our hotel. The building where we checked-in had a restaurant. Before eating lunch, we deposited our luggage in our room. All the rooms were on the ground floor and attached to each other.

After lunch, Marie-Jo and I walked to the Royallieu camp to meet the director, Mrs. Bonamy. Before entering the building, we saw several panels of glass on which were engraved thousands of names. I searched for the names of my family, but they were not there. I later found out that they were the names of 40,000 men and women who were either resistance fighters or Jews who were deported to Auschwitz or other German camps. The resistants were men and women who opposed the Germany's occupation of France during World War Two.

We entered the building and walked to the reception desk.

"Good afternoon, I'm Charlotte Trinchieri Ward and this my friend Marie-Jo Dioudonnat from Paris. Mrs. Bonamy is expecting us."

"Welcome, she said. I'll let her know that you arrived."

She introduced us to Mr. Joël Bramard whose father liberated Compiègne the 1st of September 1944. Madame Bonamy greeted us warmly. I learned that they were 25 barracks and only two barracks of Camp B remained.

I said, "What a coincidence, all the women of my family and I were interned in Camp B.

She asked me, "Do you remember these barracks?"

I answered, "I don't remember that the barracks were so large, but I remember the setting of the room."

Before we left, she reminded me that all of us were invited for dinner at noon the next day. There, we will meet all the people who made this event possible.

Heiner and Ira arrived the next day with their beautiful camper that we all admired. All four of us walked to the camp Royallieu. We were introduced to René Castellanos who in 1943 was interned at the age of 17 while I was 7 years old. Although he was a patient at the hospital, he insisted on coming. I enjoyed his presence because he had a great sense of humor.

Before entering the barrack, we were saluted by the members of the Honor Guard of the Association of Former Franco-American Combatants. We all sang the National Anthem of the United State before entering the building. Mrs. Bonamy gave us a tour of some of the displays. I was so amazed when she showed me a drawing of the American Camp of Compiègne where the women who were detained there had signed their names. My signature plus those of my grand-mother Marie, my mother Mary, my Sister Jeannine, my Aunt Jeannette and my Aunt Josephine was the biggest of them all.

It was unbelievable, so much so that when I returned home I found a letter that I had written to my high school guidance counselor when I was in France in 1952. She had sent the letter back to me because she wanted me to remember those years of my life. My signature was exactly the same.

Madame Bonamy escorted Mr. Castellanos, his wife and me to her office. Also present was Tiphaine Dupuy de Mery. She was studying for a master's degree in history and was interested in learning more about the camp of Royallieu. Mrs. Bonamy and she met. Mrs. Bonamy told her that for years she wanted to know more about the American camp. Miss Dupuy de Mery spoke to her professors who gave her permission to research the forgotten Americans about whom they knew little about.

Miss Dupuy de Mery went to Geneva and Bern, Switzerland. In the archives, she found all the information concerning the Americans, such as relations of the Suisse consulate with the Americans, of the International Red-Cross, and provisional passports. The history of these 500 Americans was there under her eyes. The Swiss government contacted the Red-Cross to make sure that we would get a box of food. I have one of the boxes at my home. They also made visits to the camp to make sure we were all right. Her research was a page of the History of World War II. As a result, the Exposition of THE FORGOTEN INTERNS – THE AMERICANS OF CAMP B OF ROYALLIEU took place from October 24, 2015 until April 25, 2016.

While there, I was interviewed by the press and by the television reporters. It was my first experience. They taught me how to answer their questions. It had to be in complete sentences. For instance, "Where were you born?" "I was born in Nice, France."

We had time to visit the displays. I took pictures so I could show my family and friends. Here is a summary of what I learned.

- One of the prisoners insulted the Germans. He had to spend one week in prison. When he was discharged, he had tuberculosis.

- Minors who were interned were protected from abuse by the Abbé Louis Comtois.
- Not all of the prisoners were treated equally. For example: the United States Government loaned money to U.S. citizens.
- Some Polish Jewish people from the ghetto of Varsovie were interned in Camp B. Because they were able to obtain South American visa.
- Dr. Summer Jackson and his son Phillip were arrested, because they were members of the Parisian network of Goelette. They were deported to the camp of Neuengamme. Phillip returned, but his father died when the ship he was on sank in the bay of Lübeck.
- Donna Hasson saved her nineteen year old son's life by informing the German commander that her son was born in Cuba and had an American visa. Her son was transferred from Camp C to Camp B which kept him from being transferred to Auschwitz. However; she, her husband Victor and her son David were deported to Auschwitz and Sobiber from where they never returned.

In the second building, there were black and white films portraying the living conditions in: Dachau, Auschwitz, Mauthaesen, Buchenwald, Ravensbrück, Neuengamme and Sachsenhousen. the filmmakers Marie-Claude Valliant-Couturier, Edmond Michelet, and Maurice Choquet. Seeing these films made me realize how lucky my family and I were to have survived.

Before giving my speech, we were invited to dinner. Present were Mrs. Bonany her staff, Tiphane Dupuy de Mery, the Honor Guard of the Association of the Franco-American

Veterans and Mr. and Mrs. Castellanos, and my friends Marie-Jo, Heiner and Ira. I sat across Mr. and Mrs. Castellanos. Mr. Castellanos mentioned that when he was admitted to the camp he had radish seeds in his pocket. He planted them and several men of his camp took turns to guard them. I also learned that he, my father, and the other men who were in Royallieu-Compiègne were transported to a crazy house in Clermont-Oise to make room for the Jewish men. Every morning, at 10 o'clock, the sound of the bugle woke them up. The camp was visited by the Swiss to verify that they were well. Mr. Castellanos also said that while in camp, he was able to continue his studies. He said that he studied commerce because he wanted to make money. I learned from him that the detainees between the ages of 16-21 were able to continue their education. The YMCA supplied a library of 500 books. Students who had already begun their studies could request specific books from the YMCA. The CICR contacted the American universities to confirm that the students had followed the curriculum. The prisoners taught each other various subjects. They scheduled five courses each day six times a week. The following foreign languages were taught: German, English, Esperanto, Italian, Latin, Russian and Spanish. In addition, they taught: accounting, algebra, chemistry, electricity, geography, literature, math, singing and technology. A library was available to the internees.

While in Compiègne, I had the pleasure to meet Danielle Dubowsky-Haddad and her brother Sylvain Dubowsky, friends of Mrs. Anne Bonamy. She and her mother, father and two brothers were prisoners in Vittel. We attended the same school, however: we didn't know each other. She told me a wonderful story about her younger brother. One day, when her family woke up, her younger brother was missing. When he returned, he said that he went to the gate of the camp to ask the guard if he could open the gate so he could know how it felt to be free. The guard who had children of his own understood the importance of his wishes and opened the gate.

During my visit, I learned many facts. I didn't know that Camp B was the only camp to benefit of individual beds with sheets and blankets. We also were privileged to have a wood burning stove. Our day began at 8 o'clock by taking a cold shower. A warm shower was permitted only once a week. After drinking a cup of tea, we had to gather for one of two inspections. The second one took place in the evening. At first, the interns were only given a piece of bread with honey and a cup of tea. No wonder the prisoners were so thin when we arrived! The conditions were clearly improved by the actions of the CICR which provided inspectors who had access to the camp in order to insure that the rules of the convention of Geneva were respected. In the event that the internes needed something the CICR came to the rescue. To celebrate Thanksgiving and Christmas, packages of real holiday food were The Americans also were allowed to send letters up to four times a month. The Americans were also able to receive visits from relatives in the parlor; however, we didn't have any relatives in France.

Before leaving, Marie-Jo, Heiner, Ira and I went to visit the American military vehicles which were displayed in the Memorial garden, thanks to the French Federation of the Conservation of Military Vehicles.

I recently found out from Mrs. Anne Bonamy that both Danielle Dubowsky-Haddad and René Castellanos have passed away. I treasure the moments I spent with them and send my sincere condolences to their families.

I want to thank Mrs. Anne Bonamy, Director of the Royallieu camp, for inviting me to speak as a representative of the 500 forgotten Americans interned in Royallieu. I also want to thank Tiphaine Dupuy de Mery because without her research, this celebration would not have taken place. I want to offer my gratitude to the Florence Gould Foundation for its financial support to set-up the displays, I want to show my appreciation to the members of the French Federation of the Conservation of Military Vehicles. And, in conclusion, I want to thank the hundreds of people who were present when I made my speech including my friends Marie-Jo, Heiner and Ira.

For years, I wondered why we were interned during the Second World War. We were used for barter. We were kept as pawns to be exchanged for German soldiers. Eleven million other individuals were not so lucky. In the atrocity of the Holocaust six million Jews and five million other individuals were not so lucky. In the atrocity of the Holocaust six million Jews and five-million non- Jews were executed. Let us not forget the horrors of wars. We as Americans should set an example to the world. Let us all live in peace.

~ FIN ~

The Wall of Names

The wall contains the names of more than 40,000 Jews and resistance fighters sent to Auschwitz

Garden of Rememberance

The Memorial of the Interment and Deportation

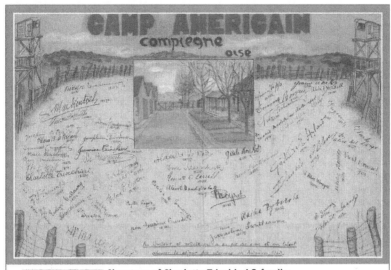

Signature of Charlotte Trinchieri & family

Interview by the Press
(Left to Right)

Tiphaine Dupuy de Mery, Anne Bonamy,
Charlotte Trinchieri Ward, and André Castellanos

Saturday, October 24, 2015 was the first time that Charlotte Trinchieri Ward returned to Royallieu Camp of Compiègne which is now known as the Memorial of the Internement and Deportation. She was 7 years old when she was interned in Camp B with her entire family, because of their American nationality. She thanked us for all we have done to recognize that we were here. She told her story to a numerous crowd. Mrs. Anne Bonamy, Director of the Memorial.

Charlotte Trinchieri, René Castellanos with the staff
of Royallieu and the honor guards.